YOUR recipe could appear in our next cookbook!

Share your tried & true family favorites with us instantly at

www.gooseberrypatch.com

If you'd rather jot 'em down by hand, just mail this form to...

Gooseberry Patch • Cookbooks – Call for Recipes
2500 Farmers Dr., #110 • Columbus, OH 43235

If your recipe is selected for a book, you'll receive a FREE copy!

Please share only your original recipes or those that you have made your own over the years.

Recipe Name:

Number of Servings:

Any fond memories about this recipe? Special touches you like to add
or handy shortcuts?

Ingredients (include specific measurements):

Instructions (continue on back if needed):

Special Code: **cookbookspage**

Over ↗

Extra space for recipe if needed:

Tell us about yourself...

Your complete contact information is needed so that we can send you your FREE cookbook, if your recipe is published. Phone numbers and email addresses are kept private and will only be used if we have questions about your recipe.

Name:

Address:

City: State: Zip:

Email:

Daytime Phone:

Thank you! Vickie & Jo Ann

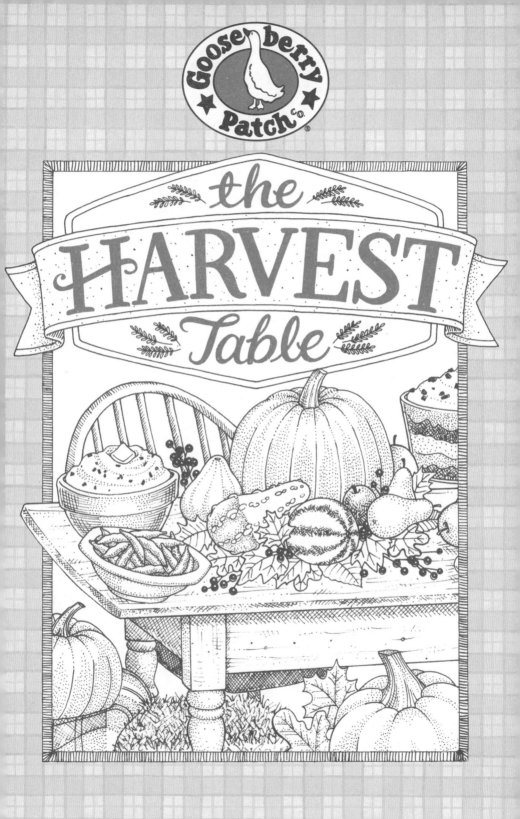

Gooseberry Patch Co.

the HARVEST Table

Gooseberry Patch
2500 Farmers Dr., #110
Columbus, OH 43235

www.gooseberrypatch.com

1·800·854·6673

Copyright 2012, Gooseberry Patch 978-1-61281-053-9
First Printing, March, 2012

Do you have a tried & true recipe...
tip, craft or memory that you'd like to see featured in a **Gooseberry
Patch** cookbook? Visit our website at **www.gooseberrypatch.com**
to share them with us instantly. If you'd rather jot them down by hand,
use the handy form in the front of this book and send them to...

Gooseberry Patch
Attn: Cookbook Dept.
2500 Farmers Dr., #110
Columbus, OH 43235

Don't forget to include the number of servings your recipe makes,
plus your name, address, phone number and email address.
If we select your recipe, your name will appear right along
with it...and you'll receive a **FREE** copy of the cookbook!

Contents

Hearty Autumn Brunch 5

Soup Supper
with Friends 37

Simple Harvest
Supper 69

Thanksgiving with
All the Trimmings 107

Festive Fall Flavors 145

Save Room for Dessert 181

Dedication

For everyone gathered around
harvest tables during this
most bountiful time of year.

Appreciation

Thanks to all our friends who
shared their most delicious recipes
and fondest autumn memories.

Hearty Autumn Brunch

Roz's Brunch Casserole

Rosalind Dickinson
Grandview, WA

My husband's family has a Thanksgiving brunch every year, and I'm required to bring this delicious dish...it's a real favorite! I love that I can dice the veggies and ham the night before, then in the morning it takes only ten minutes to pop it in the oven. Even the warmed-up leftovers taste fantastic!

1/2 c. onion, diced
1/2 c. green pepper, diced
1 to 2 t. oil
2 c. cooked ham, diced
1 doz. eggs, beaten
1 c. milk
32-oz. pkg. frozen shredded
   potatoes

1 c. shredded Cheddar cheese
seasoning salt or salt-free
   seasoning blend to taste
pepper to taste
Garnish: additional shredded
   Cheddar cheese

In a skillet over medium heat, cook onion and green pepper in oil until softened. Add ham and warm through; remove from heat. In a large bowl, stir together eggs, milk, frozen potatoes, onion mixture and cheese. Add seasonings to taste. Pour into a lightly greased 13"x9" baking pan, spreading evenly. Bake, uncovered, at 350 degrees for 45 minutes to one hour, until set. Top with additional cheese. Serves 10 to 15.

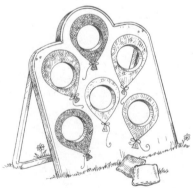

Small-town county fairs, food festivals, craft shows, swap meets...the list goes on & on, so grab a friend or two and go for good old-fashioned fun. A hearty warm breakfast will get you off to a terrific start.

Hearty Autumn
Brunch

Ursula's Breakfast Danish
Ursula Juarez-Wall
Dumfries, VA

Your company will never guess that you made these scrumptious treats in less than 30 minutes! Try filling them with fruit jam instead of cream cheese...they're great either way.

2 8-oz. tubes refrigerated
   crescent rolls
1/4 c. cream cheese, softened
1/4 t. vanilla extract

1/2 c. powdered sugar
2 to 3 t. milk
1/4 c. chopped pecans or sliced
   almonds

Unroll one tube of crescent rolls without separating rolls; press together to make one large rectangle. Repeat with remaining tube. Cut each rectangle lengthwise into 4 long strips, making 8 strips. Coil each strip into a roll while twisting it; tuck end under slightly. Arrange rolls on an greased baking sheet. With your thumb, make a slight indentation in the center of each roll. In a bowl, blend cream cheese and vanilla. Fill indentations with a teaspoon of cream cheese mixture. Bake at 375 degrees for 10 to 14 minutes, until golden. Remove to a wire rack; cool. In a separate bowl, stir together powdered sugar and enough milk to make a drizzling consistency. Drizzle rolls with glaze and sprinkle with nuts. Makes 8 rolls.

During the first week of school, deliver a tray of your favorite breakfast goodies to the teachers' lounge...they're sure to be appreciated!

Flap Jack-o'-Lanterns

Terri La Bounty
British Columbia, Canada

*Topped with maple or cinnamon syrup, these pancakes are
irresistible! Kids love to make the pumpkin faces on them.*

2 c. all-purpose flour
2 T. sugar
1 T. baking powder
1/2 t. salt
1/2 t. cinnamon
1/2 t. ground ginger
1/2 t. nutmeg

2 eggs, beaten
1-3/4 c. milk
1/2 c. canned pumpkin
2 T. butter, melted
Garnish: raisins, maple syrup
   or cinnamon syrup

In a large bowl, mix flour, sugar, baking powder, salt and spices. In a
separate bowl, whisk eggs and milk; add pumpkin and butter. Add
egg mixture to flour mixture; stir just until blended. Pour batter by
1/4 cupfuls onto a greased hot griddle or skillet. When bottom is
almost done, make a pumpkin face on top with raisins; turn. Cook
until done; serve with syrup. Serves 4.

A delicious way to perk up a bowl of oatmeal...stir in
a tablespoon or two of canned pumpkin. Top with
a sprinkle of pumpkin pie spice. Good and good-for-you!

Hearty Autumn
Brunch

Golden Banana Waffles

Tonya Adams
Magnolia, KY

These anything-but-ordinary waffles deserve to be dressed up with dollops of luscious whipped cream.

2 c. all-purpose flour
2 T. sugar
1 T. baking powder
1/4 t. salt

3 eggs, separated
1-1/4 c. milk
1 c. banana, mashed
3 T. butter, melted

Mix flour, sugar, baking powder and salt in a large bowl. In a separate bowl, beat egg yolks with milk, banana and butter until smooth. Add to flour mixture, stirring until just moistened. In another bowl, beat egg whites with an electric mixer on high speed until stiff peaks form; fold into batter. Let batter stand for 5 to 10 minutes. Add batter to a greased hot waffle iron by 1/2 cupfuls; bake according to manufacturer's instructions. Prepare Banana Topping while waffles are baking; serve over waffles. Makes about 10.

Banana Topping:

1 T. cornstarch
1/4 t. salt
1-1/2 c. apricot nectar, divided
2 T. honey

1 T. lemon juice
2 T. butter
3 bananas, sliced

In a saucepan, blend cornstarch and salt with a small amount of nectar. Gradually stir in remaining nectar and honey. Cook over low heat until thickened, stirring constantly; remove from heat. Add lemon juice and butter, stirring until butter melts. Stir in sliced bananas.

Make breakfast waffle sandwiches for a delicious change. Tuck scrambled eggs, a browned sausage patty and a slice of cheese between waffles...yum!

Scrambled Egg Muffins

Vicki Chambliss
Louisville, MS

*My children enjoy these tasty muffins for breakfast before school.
I like to make up several batches on Sunday afternoon, then
the kids can just pop them in the microwave in the morning!*

1/2 lb. ground pork sausage
1 doz. eggs, beaten
1/2 c. onion, chopped
1/2 c. green pepper, chopped
1/4 t. garlic powder

1/2 t. salt
1/4 t. pepper
1/2 c. shredded sharp Cheddar
   cheese

Brown sausage in a skillet over medium heat; drain well. In a bowl,
whisk together eggs, onion, green pepper and seasonings. Stir in
sausage and cheese. Spoon into greased muffin cups by 1/3 cupfuls.
Bake at 350 degrees for 20 to 25 minutes, until a knife tip inserted in
the center tests clean. Serve warm. Makes 6 to 8.

Layer creamy low-fat yogurt, fresh berries and crunchy
whole-grain cereal in old-fashioned parfait or sundae glasses...
so easy for brunch guests to help themselves! Chill glasses in
the freezer before filling so they'll stay frosty longer.

Hearty Autumn
Brunch

Brown Sugar Muffins

Doris Carrig
Miami, FL

*I have 14 grandchildren, and when they come for breakfast
at my house, they all love these yummy muffins!*

1 c. quick-cooking oats,
   uncooked
1/2 c. milk
3/4 c. brown sugar, packed
1/4 c. butter, melted and slightly
   cooled

1 egg, beaten
1 c. all-purpose flour
1/2 c. chopped walnuts
2 t. baking powder

Mix oats, milk and brown sugar in a large bowl; let stand for
5 minutes. Add butter and egg; blend well. Stir in remaining
ingredients just until moistened. Fill greased muffin cups 2/3 full. Bake
at 400 degrees for 15 to 20 minutes, until a toothpick inserted in the
center comes out clean. Makes one dozen.

In our home, we have a saying that when something isn't perfect,
or has been damaged, it's not really broken, it's just "loved."
When my little girl Victoria was in kindergarten, she took her first
class trip to the pumpkin patch. I went along as a chaperone. The
teachers told all the children they could pick out any pumpkin
they wanted to take home. Most children searched for a perfectly
shaped, unblemished pumpkin. My daughter carefully looked
over the pumpkins and without hesitation she picked up a little
lopsided, scratched pumpkin. She brought it up to me
and said, "Look at the pumpkin I picked, Mommy, it looks like
it's been loved...just like me!" My heart melted. We took that
little pumpkin home, carved it and put it near the fireplace
for all to see, and it was indeed loved.

–Melissa Varela, Clovis, CA

Mom's Buttermilk Pancakes
Debbie Driggers
Campbell, TX

When I was growing up, we always looked forward to Sunday nights after church. That's when my mom would serve these pancakes for supper with her own special syrup.

2 c. buttermilk
3 eggs, beaten
2 T. oil
1/2 c. evaporated milk
1/2 t. vanilla extract
1 T. sugar

1 T. baking powder
1 T. baking soda
1/2 t. salt
1 t. active dry yeast
2 c. all-purpose flour

In a large bowl, combine all ingredients; whisk well. Pour 1/3 cup batter onto a hot greased griddle for each pancake. Cook until top of each pancake is speckled with bubbles; turn and cook until other side is lightly golden. Serve warm pancakes with Homemade Maple Syrup. Makes 10 to 12.

Homemade Maple Syrup:

1 c. water
2 c. sugar

1/4 t. maple flavoring

In a small saucepan over medium-high heat, bring water to a boil. Add sugar; stir until completely dissolved and clear. Stir in maple flavoring. Cool; store in a covered container.

Make a scrumptious apple topping for pancakes and waffles. Sauté 3 cups sliced apples in a tablespoon of butter over medium-high heat until tender, about 8 minutes. Stir in 1/4 cup maple syrup and sprinkle with 1/2 teaspoon cinnamon. Serve warm.

Hearty Autumn
Brunch

Mashed Potato Doughnuts

Diane Meyer
Marion, IA

This is my Grama's recipe...my mom and I made these wonderful doughnuts and now the fourth generation is making them too. They're well worth the effort!

1 c. plain mashed potatoes
1 c. sugar
2 eggs, beaten
1/2 c. milk
1/2 t. vanilla extract
3-1/2 c. all-purpose flour

4 t. baking powder
1/2 t. cinnamon
1/2 t. nutmeg
canola oil for frying
Garnish: cinnamon-sugar

In a large bowl, mix together mashed potatoes and sugar; stir in eggs, milk and vanilla. Add flour, baking powder and spices; mix well. Roll out dough on a floured surface about 1/2-inch thick; cut with a doughnut cutter. In a large skillet, heat several inches of oil until hot. Fry several doughnuts at a time, turning them over as they become golden. Doughnut holes and any scraps of dough may be fried also. Drain on paper towels; sprinkle with cinnamon-sugar while still hot. Store doughnuts in an airtight container. Makes 3 dozen.

Pull out all your favorites to welcome autumn! Fill your open cupboards with brown crocks, redware bowls, gourds, bundles of wheat and sweet-scented beeswax candles. Line shelves with quilts or folded lengths of homespun in warm autumn colors.

Jo Ann's Garden Frittata

Jo Ann

Family & friends are sure to love this savory egg dish.
It's filled with brightly colored vegetables...beautiful to
look at and delicious to eat.

4 thick slices bacon, chopped
1 onion, diced
1 red pepper, thinly sliced
1 c. corn
1 c. green beans, thinly sliced
1 bunch Swiss chard, thinly
    sliced

3 eggs, beaten
1-1/4 c. half-and-half
1/8 t. dried thyme
salt and pepper to taste
1 c. shredded Cheddar cheese

In a large oven-proof skillet over medium-high heat, cook bacon
until crisp. Drain bacon on paper towels; reserve drippings. In one
tablespoon drippings, sauté onion, red pepper and corn for 5 minutes.
Add beans; sauté another 3 minutes. Transfer vegetable mixture to a
bowl; set aside. Add one teaspoon drippings to skillet; sauté chard for
2 minutes. Add to vegetable mixture in bowl. In a separate large bowl,
whisk eggs, half-and-half and seasonings. Stir in bacon, cheese and
vegetable mixture; pour into skillet. Bake at 375 degrees for about
35 minutes, until set and crust is golden. Let stand for 10 minutes;
cut into wedges. Makes 8 servings.

A handy memo-keeper that's ready in a jiffy! Hang a
cast-iron skillet on a sturdy hook; then use magnets to
hold grocery lists, coupons and back-to-school notes.

Hearty Autumn
Brunch

Italian Scramble

Kathleen Kennedy
Renton, WA

My adaption of a favorite restaurant's late-night offering. Use hot or mild sausage, or a combination of the two.

8 eggs, beaten
1/4 c. half-and-half or milk
1 lb. Italian pork sausage links, casings removed

1/2 c. fresh spinach, chopped
pepper to taste
Garnish: shredded Parmesan cheese

In a bowl, whisk together eggs and half-and-half or milk; set aside. Brown sausage in a large skillet over medium-high heat, breaking it up as it cooks; drain. Add egg mixture to sausage in skillet; reduce heat to medium-low. Cook until eggs start to set. Add spinach and pepper. Cook, stirring occasionally, until eggs are set. Sprinkle with Parmesan cheese before serving. Serves 4.

Enjoy a worn-out quilt again by turning it into a table topper. Cut the quilt to the desired size, then stack with cotton batting and backing fabric cut to the same size. Stitch together around the edges and finish with extra-wide double-fold bias tape.

Wilderness Breakfast

Tammy Adam
Lathrop, MO

This recipe was handed down from my Great-Uncle Russell. He used to cook this breakfast dish while camping on long hunting trips with his sons. My own daughters have used this recipe for 4-H demonstrations and been very successful with it. It can be prepared the night before, refrigerated and baked the next morning.

3 c. croutons
1-1/2 c. shredded Cheddar
   cheese
6 to 8 eggs, beaten
3 c. milk
10-3/4 oz. can cream of chicken
   soup
3/4 t. dried, minced onion

3/4 t. dry mustard
3/4 t. salt
1/8 t. pepper
1 lb. bacon, crisply cooked and
   crumbled
1 lb. ground pork sausage,
   browned and drained

Line a greased 13"x9" baking pan with croutons and cheese; set aside. In a large bowl, stir together eggs, milk, soup, onion, mustard, salt and pepper. Pour mixture over croutons and cheese; sprinkle with bacon and sausage. Bake, uncovered, for one hour at 325 degrees. Serves 6 to 8.

Bacon-Fried Spiced Apples

James Bohner
Harrisburg, PA

Make this sweet & salty side after frying your bacon. It's delicious on a breakfast platter or spooned over a bowl of oatmeal.

2 T. bacon drippings
2 apples, cored and sliced into
   rings

1/3 c. brown sugar, packed
1 t. cinnamon

Warm bacon drippings in a skillet over medium heat. Add apples and cook for 2 minutes. Sprinkle brown sugar and cinnamon over apples. Turn over; continue cooking for one to 2 minutes, until apples are tender and golden. Serves 4 to 6.

Hearty Autumn Brunch

Camp-Time Eggs & Bacon

Tina George
El Dorado, AR

For five years I was a counselor at our church's Bible camp. I always looked forward to eating these eggs for breakfast. Serve them with crisp hashbrowns and buttered toast...perfect!

1 lb. bacon
1 doz. eggs, beaten
1/2 c. milk

2 T. margarine, divided
1/2 to 1 c. shredded Cheddar
  cheese

In a non-stick skillet over medium heat, cook bacon until crisp. Drain bacon on a paper towel-covered plate; drain skillet. Cut bacon into 1/2-inch pieces and set aside. In a bowl, beat eggs with milk until well blended. Add one tablespoon margarine to skillet; stir until melted. Add egg mixture; cook over medium heat until eggs are set, stirring occasionally to scramble. Turn off heat. Add bacon and desired amount of cheese; stir until cheese melts. Serves 10 to 12.

Go out to greet the sunrise! Wrap warm breakfast breads
in a vintage tea towel before tucking into a basket...
add a thermos of hot coffee or tea.

Crumb Coffee Cake
Deanna Polito-Laughinghouse
Knightdale, NC

I'm from New Jersey and grew up on this fabulous coffee cake that has more crumb topping than cake! Now I live in North Carolina, and for 20 years I haven't been able to find this delectable cake anywhere. So, I created a recipe for it...this way I can enjoy a piece of coffee cake whenever I want!

1/2 c. butter, softened	2 c. all-purpose flour
1-1/3 c. sugar	2 t. baking powder
2 eggs, beaten	1-1/2 t. vanilla extract
3/4 c. low-fat milk	Garnish: 1/2 c. powdered sugar

Line a 13"x9" baking pan with non-stick aluminum foil; set aside. In a large bowl, blend butter and sugar. Stir in eggs and milk; set aside. In a separate bowl, mix flour and baking powder; add flour mixture to butter mixture. Add vanilla; beat until combined. Pour batter into prepared pan. Sprinkle Crumb Topping over cake batter with your hands, squeezing it together as you do. Crumb Topping should be lumpy; there will be more topping than cake. Bake at 350 degrees for 40 minutes. Cool for 15 to 20 minutes; top with powdered sugar. Makes 16 servings.

Crumb Topping:

6 c. biscuit baking mix	5 to 6 t. cinnamon
2 c. sugar	1-1/2 c. margarine
1 c. brown sugar, packed	

Combine biscuit mix, sugars and cinnamon in a large bowl. Cut in margarine; combine with your hands until well mixed.

A vintage-style wire basket full of brown eggs makes a charming centerpiece on the breakfast table.

Peach Butter Muffins

Violet Leonard
Chesapeake, VA

I make my own home-canned peach butter every summer and use it to make these muffins all winter long. You can make this recipe using apple butter instead. Yummy!

1-3/4 c. all-purpose flour
1/3 c. sugar
2 t. baking powder
1 t. pumpkin or apple pie spice
1 egg, beaten

1/2 c. milk
1/4 c. oil
1/4 c. plus 1/3 c. peach butter, divided
Garnish: cinnamon-sugar

In a large bowl, combine flour, sugar, baking powder and spice. Make a well in the center and set aside. In a separate bowl, whisk together egg, milk, oil and 1/4 cup peach butter; pour into well in flour mixture. Stir just until moistened. Spoon a rounded tablespoon of batter into each of 12 paper-lined muffin cups. Top each with a rounded teaspoon of remaining peach butter; divide remaining batter among muffin cups. Sprinkle with cinnamon-sugar. Bake at 350 degrees for 20 to 25 minutes, or until set. Best served warm. Makes one dozen.

Every autumn when apples were ready to pick at the nearby orchard, our neighbor Mac would call ahead and arrange for my family to pick fallen apples off the ground and get them half-price. We loaded every box, bucket and crate into the van for the kids and me to fill. Sometimes Mac came along with us to help. Back home, we would peel and slice, filling up every slow cooker with apples, a cup of sugar and a touch of cinnamon. The whole house smelled sweetly of apples! Mac passed away on Valentine's Day 2011. We miss our dear neighbor so much, but with every taste of apple we remember him fondly.

–Lorraine Bretzin, Rixeyville, VA

Goetta Breakfast Sausage

Patrick Benesch
Saint Petersburg, FL

A German recipe passed down from my family on my dad's side since 1806. Our motto is, "It's good anytime...gotta get our Goetta!"

8 c. water
2-1/2 c. pinhead or steel-cut
    oats, uncooked
1 T. salt
1-1/2 t. pepper, or to taste

1 lb. ground beef
1 lb. ground pork or pork
    sausage
1 onion, sliced
Optional: 1 to 4 bay leaves

In a large stockpot, combine water, oats, salt and pepper. Bring to a boil over high heat. Reduce heat to medium-low; cover and simmer for 2 hours. Crumble in meats; add onion and bay leaves, if using. Cover and cook for another hour, stirring occasionally. Discard bay leaves. Pour mixture into an ungreased 9"x5" loaf pan; cool. Cover and refrigerate up to 2 weeks, or freeze until ready to use. To serve, turn loaf out of pan and cut into thin slices. Cook slices in a little butter or oil until crisp and golden on both sides. Serves 6 to 8.

Slow-Cooker Method:

Heat water, salt and pepper in a slow cooker. Add oats; cover and cook on high setting for 1-1/2 hours. Add remaining ingredients. Turn heat to low; cover and cook an additional 3 hours. If too thin, uncover and cook a little longer until thickened. Pour into a loaf pan and proceed as directed above.

With the holidays coming, fall is an excellent time to check your spice rack. Take a pinch of each spice and crush it between your fingers. If it has a fresh, zingy scent, it's still fine to use. Toss out old-smelling spices and stock up on any that you've used up during the year.

Hearty Autumn
Brunch

Glorious Cheese Grits

Angela Matos
Ocoee, FL

We southern girls know a thing or two about grits...my recipe really dresses them up. I have taken it to several covered-dish functions and so many people ask what it is, because they have never had grits this yummy before! You're gonna love every spoonful.

4 c. water
1 c. long-cooking grits, uncooked
3 c. shredded sharp Cheddar cheese, divided
2 T. butter

1-1/2 t. garlic salt
1 t. Worcestershire sauce
1 egg, beaten
1 lb. pork breakfast sausage, browned and drained

In a large saucepan, bring water to a boil over high heat. Stir in grits; bring to a second boil. Reduce heat; cover and cook for 5 minutes, stirring occasionally. Remove from heat. Add 2 cups cheese, butter, garlic salt and Worcestershire sauce; mix thoroughly until cheese is melted. Stir egg slowly into mixture. Transfer half of mixture to a buttered 2-quart casserole dish. Add cooked sausage; top with remaining grits mixture. Cover and refrigerate at least 8 hours. To serve, let stand at room temperature for 30 minutes. Bake, uncovered, at 350 degrees for 40 minutes. Remove from oven and top with remaining cheese. Return to oven for several minutes, until cheese is melted. Makes 4 to 6 servings.

Serve a variety of cheeses at your brunch...perfect for guests to nibble on! Arrange brightly colored autumn leaves on a clear glass plate, then top with another glass plate to hold them in place. Fill with assorted cheeses, crackers and crisp apple slices.

Jane's Sweet Bubble Bread   *JoAnn*

This tasty recipe came from an old friend of mine. She was close to retirement age years ago when we taught school together.

1/2 c. butter, melted
1-1/2 c. sugar
1-1/2 t. cinnamon
2 16-oz. loaves frozen bread
   dough, thawed

1 c. chopped nuts, divided
2 T. dark corn syrup, divided

Place melted butter in a small bowl; mix cinnamon and sugar in a separate small bowl. Form dough into walnut-size balls; roll in butter, then in cinnamon-sugar. Place half of dough balls in a greased Bundt® pan. Sprinkle with 1/4 cup nuts; drizzle with one tablespoon corn syrup. Pack remaining dough balls on top. Sprinkle with 1/4 cup nuts; drizzle with remaining corn syrup. Cover and let rise until dough doubles in size. Bake at 350 degrees for 25 minutes. Cool for 3 minutes; invert onto a serving plate and top with remaining nuts. Makes 10 to 12 servings.

Pumpkin Spice Latte   *Kim Wilson*
Melbourne, FL

I love to buy lattes at my favorite coffee place but it can get very expensive. So here is a homemade version with ingredients you probably already have on hand. Enjoy!

3 c. hot milk
2 T. sugar
1/2 t. vanilla extract
1 t. pumpkin pie spice

1 c. hot strong brewed coffee
Garnish: whipped cream,
   pumpkin pie spice

Combine hot milk, sugar, vanilla and spice in a blender. Process until frothy. Pour into 3 to 4 coffee mugs, filling 2/3 full. Divide coffee among mugs. Garnish mugs with a dollop of whipped cream and a sprinkle of pumpkin pie spice. Serves 3 to 4.

Classic Quiche Lorraine

Francie Stutzman
Clinton, OH

*This recipe makes two delicious quiches...just add a fresh fruit salad
for an oh-so-easy brunch with friends.*

1 lb. bacon, cut into 1-inch
  pieces
2 9-inch pie crusts
8-oz. pkg. shredded Swiss
  cheese
8-oz. pkg. shredded Cheddar
  cheese

8 eggs, beaten
2 c. whipping cream
1 T. Worcestershire sauce
1/8 t. salt
1 T. pepper

In a skillet over medium-high heat, cook bacon until crisp; drain on
paper towels. Arrange pie crusts in two 9-inch pie plates; sprinkle
bacon into crusts. Mix together cheeses in a bowl; sprinkle over bacon.
In a separate bowl, whisk together remaining ingredients. Divide egg
mixture between the crusts. Bake at 350 degrees for 45 minutes, or
until golden. Let stand about 10 minutes; cut into wedges and serve
warm. Makes 2 quiches; each serves 6.

Make 'em mini! Bake a favorite quiche recipe in mini
muffin cups for individual servings...just decrease baking time
by 10 to 15 minutes. Top each bite-size quiche with
a dainty dollop of sour cream and a sprig of dill.

Little Tot's Tater Breakfast

Vanessa Malone
Magnolia, AR

One day, my 4-year-old son Ethan wanted potato puffs for breakfast, so I decided to combine eggs with them. I named it Little Tot's because he tasted it and said, "This is great!" My husband is from Louisiana, where we lived for ten years, so hot sauce is a must when we fix eggs. But heat doesn't deter my sons at all! Your kids will say, "Yummy!"

12-oz. pkg. maple-flavored pork breakfast sausages, cut into bite-size pieces
1 onion, diced
2 cloves garlic, minced
8 eggs, beaten
1/4 c. whipping cream or half-and-half
1 t. to 1 T. hot pepper sauce
salt and pepper to taste
3 c. frozen potato puffs
8-oz. pkg. shredded Mexican-blend cheese
Garnish: catsup

In a skillet over medium-high heat, cook sausage until browned; drain. Add onion and garlic to skillet; cook until tender. Remove from heat. In a bowl, whisk together eggs, cream or half-and-half, hot sauce, salt and pepper; set aside. In a lightly greased 13"x9" baking pan, layer frozen potato puffs and sausage mixture; pour egg mixture evenly over top. Bake, uncovered, at 350 degrees for 35 minutes, or until eggs are almost set. Sprinkle cheese on top; return to oven for another 10 minutes. Serve with catsup. Makes 6 to 8 servings.

Whip up some birdseed bagels so the birds can enjoy breakfast as the season turns chilly...fun for kids to do! Just spread peanut butter on the cut side of a bagel and coat with birdseed. Slip a length of raffia through the bagel's hole and hang from a tree outside your window.

Sunny-Side-Up Egg Pizza

Gladys Kielar
Perrysburg, OH

When you call the family for breakfast, say, "Pizza's ready!" You have to try this one. It is a delight to see and taste.

12-inch Italian pizza crust
6 eggs
1-1/2 c. shredded mozzarella
   cheese
8 slices bacon, crisply cooked
   and crumbled

1/2 c. red pepper, chopped
1/2 c. green pepper, chopped
1/2 c. onion, chopped

Place crust on a lightly greased 12" round pizza pan. With a 2-1/2" round biscuit cutter, cut out 6 circles from crust, evenly spaced and about one inch from the edge. Reserve cut-out crust circles for another use. Break an egg into each hole in the crust. Sprinkle remaining ingredients over the crust. Bake at 450 degrees for 8 to 10 minutes, until eggs are completely set. Cut into wedges. Makes 6 servings.

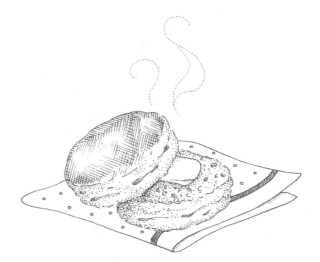

Need a biscuit cutter and you don't have one handy?
Use a small glass tumbler or the open end of
an empty soup can instead.

Bacon & Chile Quiche

Darlene Weathers-Gast
Fairfield, CA

This quiche is our favorite for holiday brunches. You can use diced ham instead of bacon. I also like to add fresh asparagus. May be made a day ahead and reheated when needed.

4 eggs, beaten
1-1/2 c. milk
4-oz. can diced green chiles,
   drained
1/2 t. salt
1/8 t. cayenne pepper

8-oz. pkg. shredded Cheddar or
   Swiss cheese
1 T. all-purpose flour
8 slices bacon, chopped and
   crisply cooked
10-inch pie crust

In a bowl, combine eggs, milk, chiles and seasonings; mix well. In a separate bowl, toss cheese with flour. Add cheese mixture and bacon to egg mixture; stir. Pour into unbaked pie crust. Bake at 350 degrees for 40 to 45 minutes. Let stand 10 minutes before cutting into wedges. Serves 6.

Planning a midday brunch? Alongside breakfast foods like baked eggs, coffee cake and cereal, offer a light, savory casserole or a zingy salad for those who have already enjoyed breakfast.

Hearty Autumn
Brunch

Amazing Tomato Omelet
Adam Gelbard
Aiea, HI

I love making this for my boys' breakfast on lazy mornings. I serve it with whole-grain wheat toast. These tomatoes can also be used for making homemade bruschetta or other Italian dishes.

5 eggs, beaten
1/3 c. onion, finely diced
1/3 c. green pepper, diced
1 c. Oven-Roasted Tomatoes, divided

1/4 c. shredded Swiss cheese
1/4 c. shredded Monterey Jack cheese
2 T. butter

In a bowl, whisk together eggs, onion, pepper and 3/4 cup Oven-Roasted Tomatoes. Add most of cheeses, reserving a little for the top. Melt butter in a non-stick skillet over medium-low heat. Add egg mixture. Cook, lifting sides to allow uncooked portion to run underneath. When omelet is done, slowly roll it out of the pan onto a plate. Top with remaining tomatoes and cheese. Serves 2 to 4.

Oven-Roasted Tomatoes:

6 roma tomatoes, quartered lengthwise

1/4 c. oil
3 cloves garlic, finely chopped

Combine all ingredients in a bowl; toss together. Spread on an ungreased baking sheet. Bake at 400 degrees for 25 to 30 minutes, until lightly caramelized. Let cool.

Line a vintage tin lunchbox with a pretty tea towel and fill with muffins or other baked goods... perfect for a back-to-school buffet!

Company Pecan French Toast
Kristen Lewis
Bourbonnais, IL

This recipe makes its own ooey-gooey caramel topping! Since you prepare it the night before, it's a convenient make-ahead when you have guests coming for brunch.

1 c. brown sugar, packed
1/2 c. margarine, melted
1 t. cinnamon
1/2 c. chopped pecans
12 slices bread

5 eggs, beaten
1-1/2 c. milk
1 t. salt
Optional: maple syrup

In a bowl, combine brown sugar, margarine, cinnamon and pecans. Spread in a greased 13"x9" glass baking pan; layer with bread slices. Whisk together eggs, milk and salt; pour over bread. Cover and refrigerate 8 hours to overnight. Uncover; bake at 350 degrees for 45 minutes to one hour. Turn slices over to serve gooey-side up. Serve with syrup, if desired. Serves 10 to 12.

Snowy paper-white narcissus flowers are a winter delight, and they're easy to grow. Place paper-white bulbs pointed-side up in water-filled bulb vases. Set in a sunny window...in about six weeks you'll have blooms!

Hearty Autumn Brunch

Sweet Blintz Soufflé

Lori Rosenberg
University Heights, OH

Mom always pulled this yummy recipe out for company and holidays. It's light, refreshing and unusual.

12 frozen blintzes, any variety
4 eggs, beaten
1/4 c. sugar
1/8 t. salt
1 t. vanilla extract
1/2 c. butter, melted and slightly cooled
1-1/2 c. sour cream
Garnish: applesauce or sour cream

Arrange frozen blintzes folded-side down in a 13"x9" glass baking pan coated with non-stick vegetable spray. In a bowl, beat eggs, sugar, salt and vanilla together; stir in butter and sour cream. Spoon over blintzes. Bake, uncovered, at 350 degrees for 40 to 45 minutes, until golden. Serve with applesauce or sour cream. Serves 6.

Sausage Balls

Joanna Watson-Donahue
Lubbock, TX

My mom and I have made this tasty recipe for many family gatherings, including the morning after my wedding. It's so simple and takes only three ingredients.

16-oz. pkg. ground pork breakfast sausage
1 c. all-purpose flour
16-oz. pkg. shredded sharp Cheddar, Pepper Jack or mozzarella cheese

Combine all ingredients in a large bowl. Knead together until completely incorporated. Form mixture into one to 1-1/2 inch balls. Place balls on parchment paper-lined baking sheets, one inch apart. Bake at 350 degrees for 15 to 20 minutes, until golden and and sausage is no longer pink. Cool slightly before serving. May be baked, then refrigerated up to one week in a plastic zipping bag and warmed at serving time. Makes 3 to 4 dozen.

Farmhouse Sausage Gravy

Laurie Harris
College Station, TX

A family favorite hearty breakfast!

1 lb. ground pork sausage	salt and pepper to taste
1/2 c. butter	3 c. milk
1/2 c. all-purpose flour	8 warm biscuits, split

In a skillet, cook sausage over medium heat until no longer pink; drain. Add butter to sausage in skillet; heat until melted. Sprinkle sausage mixture with flour, salt and pepper; cook and stir until flour is blended and starting to turn golden. Gradually add milk, stirring constantly. Bring to a boil; cook and stir for 2 minutes, or until thickened. Serve gravy over warm biscuits. Makes 8 servings.

Every autumn when I was little, I'd go to the cornfield with my Gramps and we would cut down some cornstalks. My Granny would take me to the garden where we picked Indian corn, gourds and pumpkins together. Gramps would tie up the cornstalks around the utility pole in the yard with baling twine and add a couple of bales of hay. Then I would stack the other fall items we'd gathered around the hay bales. There was always a photo taken at the end...Gramps in his overalls with his walking stick, Granny holding me and at least one pesky farm cat nearby!

–Sarah Smith, Marengo, IA

Hearty Autumn
Brunch

Poached Eggs & Grits

Pamela Stump
Chino Hills, CA

Being raised down south, for me nothing beats poached eggs and grits...one of my ultimate comfort foods!

5-1/2 c. water
1/2 t. salt
1-1/2 c. quick-cooking grits, uncooked
2 T. butter
1/3 c. finely shredded Parmigiano Reggiano cheese
1/4 c. green onions, finely chopped
4 slices bacon, crisply cooked and crumbled
pepper to taste
8 eggs

Combine water and salt in a medium saucepan over high heat; bring to a boil. Gradually whisk in grits. Reduce heat to low. Cover and cook, whisking often, until thick and creamy. Stir in remaining ingredients except eggs; cook 5 minutes longer. Meanwhile, to poach eggs, add 2 inches water to a skillet. Bring to a simmer over high heat. Break eggs into a cup, one at a time, and slide into simmering water. Cook eggs for 3 minutes. To serve, spoon grits into 4 bowls. With a slotted spoon, top each bowl with 2 eggs. Serves 4.

Spice up an autumn breakfast with cider-glazed sausages. Brown and drain 1/2 pound of breakfast sausage links. Add a cup of apple cider to the skillet, then turn the heat down to low and simmer for 10 minutes. Yummy!

Cranberry-Nut Coffee Cake

Tina Hengen
Clarkston, WA

I bake this make-ahead coffee cake every Thanksgiving and Christmas Eve. My family really looks forward to this treat. In the morning it's easy to just pop it into the oven, bake and serve warm. It makes a yummy cake even without the cranberries, if you prefer.

2 c. all-purpose flour
1 t. baking powder
1 t. baking soda
1/2 t. salt
1 t. cinnamon
1 c. butter
1 c. sugar

1/2 c. brown sugar, packed
2 eggs
1 c. Bulgarian or regular
   buttermilk
Optional: 1 c. sweetened dried
   cranberries

In a bowl, stir together flour, baking powder, baking soda, salt and cinnamon; set aside. In a separate large bowl, blend together butter and sugars; add eggs, one at a time. Add buttermilk and flour mixture alternately to butter mixture, stirring well. Mix in cranberries, if using. Spread batter evenly in a greased 13"x9" baking pan; sprinkle with Streusel Topping. Cover and refrigerate 8 hours to overnight. In the morning, bake at 350 degrees for about 45 minutes, or until a toothpick inserted in the center comes out clean. Cut into squares. Serves 12.

Streusel Topping:

1/2 c. brown sugar, packed
1/2 c. chopped pecans

1 t. cinnamon
1/4 t. nutmeg

Stir together in a small bowl.

Cloth napkins are so much nicer than paper ones...why not whip up some fun napkin rings for them? Stitch a big vintage button or a pretty silk flower onto colorful new hair elastics...done in a snap!

Hearty Autumn
Brunch

Mom's Orange Bow Knots

Katie Majeske
Denver, PA

I still love going home to find these amazing rolls in Mom's kitchen!
The recipe goes back a few generations in my family. Quick breads
may be easier, but nothing tastes better than yeast bread.

1-1/4 c. milk	2 eggs, beaten
1/2 c. shortening	1/4 c. orange juice
1/3 c. sugar	2 T. orange zest
3/4 t. salt	5 c. all-purpose flour, divided
1 env. active dry yeast	

Heat milk just to boiling. In a bowl, combine milk, shortening, sugar
and salt; let cool to about 110 to 115 degrees. Dissolve yeast in milk
mixture. Add eggs, orange juice and orange zest; beat well. Stir in
2 cups flour; let stand 10 minutes. Stir in remaining flour. Cover with
a tea towel; let rise until doubled, one to 2 hours. Punch down dough;
roll out 1/2-inch thick on a floured surface. Cut into 10-inch by
1/2-inch strips. Tie each strip loosely in a bow; arrange on lightly
greased baking sheets. Cover and let rise again, 30 minutes to one
hour. Bake at 375 degrees for 15 minutes, or until golden. Cool;
spread with Orange Frosting. Makes 2 to 3 dozen.

Orange Frosting:

2 T. orange juice	1 c. powdered sugar
1 t. orange zest	

Stir together ingredients, adding powdered sugar to desired
consistency.

Autumn's resting on the hills.
Harvested are fruit and grain,
And the home with gladness thrills.
Buckwheat cakes are back again!

–Edgar A. Guest

Nutty Skillet Granola

Gail Blain Prather
Hastings, NE

I've been making my own granola for years, but I never knew how quick & easy it could really be until I tried this speedy version!

1 c. quick-cooking oats,
    uncooked
1 c. old-fashioned oats,
    uncooked
1 c. sliced almonds
1/2 c. chopped walnuts

1/2 c. chopped pecans
1/2 c. wheat germ
1/4 c. oil
1/2 c. maple syrup
3/4 c. light brown sugar, packed
1 c. raisins

In a large bowl, mix oats, nuts and wheat germ; set aside. In a large skillet over medium heat, combine oil, maple syrup and brown sugar. Cook, stirring constantly, until sugar melts and mixture just begins to bubble, about 3 minutes. Add oat mixture; stir well to coat completely. Reduce heat to medium-low. Cook, stirring occasionally, until mixture begins to sizzle and toast, about 3 to 4 minutes; be careful not to burn. Remove from heat; stir in raisins. Cool for 10 minutes; transfer to an airtight container. Will keep for up to 2 weeks. Makes about 7 cups.

When a free morning with girlfriends means craft fair browsing or flea market shopping, scoop some tasty homemade granola into easy-to-tote sports bottles...ideal for breakfast on the road.

Hearty Autumn
Brunch

Ruby's B&B Spinach Quiche

Ruby Pruitt
Nashville, IN

When I ran a bed & breakfast, I used to serve this crustless quiche and all my guests loved it. Often they requested the recipe... some even wrote to ask after they'd returned home!

1 c. all-purpose flour
1 t. baking powder
1 t. salt
1 c. milk
2 eggs, beaten
1/4 c. onion, chopped

10-oz. pkg. frozen spinach, thawed and drained
3 T. butter, melted
8-oz. pkg. shredded sharp Cheddar cheese

Mix all ingredients together in a bowl. Pour into a 9"x9" baking pan sprayed with non-stick vegetable spray. Bake at 325 degrees for 30 to 35 minutes, until lightly golden on top. Cut into squares; serve warm. Makes 6 servings.

Host a casual outdoor breakfast for family & friends...perfect for a sunny game day! Toss stadium blankets over tables and serve baskets of warm muffins, fresh fruit, homemade jams and creamy butter. Pint-size bottles of juice and milk can be kept cold in an ice-filled galvanized bucket.

Pumpkin Hollow Surprise

Tiffani Schulte
Wyandotte, MI

I grew up on a pumpkin farm and we gave this recipe to visitors thousands of times over. You just cannot go wrong with it...and the way it makes your house smell is just incredible! I tell people to be as creative with the fillings as they like. It makes a beautiful centerpiece for a Thanksgiving brunch.

5 to 7-lb. pie pumpkin
1 to 2 T. oil
2/3 c. raisins, golden raisins or
   currants
2/3 c. sweetened dried
   cranberries

4 apples, cored and chopped
2/3 c. chopped pecans or
   walnuts
1 t. pumpkin pie spice
1/2 to 1 c. brown sugar, packed

Cut the top from the pumpkin; scoop out seeds. Place pumpkin on a baking sheet covered with aluminum foil. Rub oil lightly over the outside of the pumpkin and its lid; set aside. In a large bowl, combine fruit and nuts. Add spice and brown sugar. Depending upon the size of your pumpkin you may not need as much fruit, or you may need to add some extra fruit to fill it. Spoon fruit mixture into the pumpkin; set the lid next to it. Bake at 325 degrees for about 30 to 45 minutes, until apples are tender. Scoop out the baked pumpkin flesh and serve alongside the fruit mixture. Makes quite a few servings, depending on the size of the pumpkin.

Buy extra pie pumpkins at Halloween and store them in a cool, dry place like a garage. Keep them off the floor, with plenty of air circulating around them... your pumpkins should keep until Thanksgiving.

Soup Supper
with
Friends

Indian Corn Stew

Susan Jacobs
Vista, CA

My mom used to make this hearty soup whenever our family went camping, right after we set up camp. Nowadays we like it on a chilly night. The crusty bread is perfect for dipping in the stew. Leftovers are great warmed up for lunch the next day.

1 lb. bacon, cut into 1-inch
   pieces
1 onion, chopped
28-oz. can stewed tomatoes
29-oz. can tomato sauce
2 15-oz. cans cut green beans,
   drained

2 15-oz. cans corn, drained
pepper to taste
2 c. shredded Cheddar cheese
Garnish: crusty bread, butter
Optional: hot pepper sauce
   to taste

In a large saucepan over medium-high heat, cook bacon until crisp; drain most of drippings. Add onion; reduce heat to medium and cook until tender. Add undrained tomatoes, tomato sauce, beans, corn and pepper; heat through. To serve, ladle into 6 soup bowls and top with cheese. Serve with crusty bread, butter and hot sauce, if desired. Serves 6.

When I was growing up, my mom and I would build
our own scarecrows as a front-door decoration for the fall.
We would use my dad's worn-out flannel shirts and jeans and
anything else that just seemed perfect. It was such a fun way
to be creative and spend time together. This year my three and
four-year-old boys will help us. I'm looking forward to
making the same sweet memories with them!

–Carolyn Bingham, Columbus, GA

Soup Supper with
Friends

Bean & Butternut Soup

Jill Duvendack
Pioneer, OH

Autumn means a drive in the country to a farm market, then home to make soup. Remember to set the beans to soak ahead of time.

1 lb. dried navy beans
8 c. water
8 t. ham soup base
1 lb. meaty ham shanks
1 c. onion, chopped

1 c. celery, chopped
2 lbs. butternut squash, peeled,
cubed and divided
pepper to taste
salt to taste

In a 5-quart Dutch oven, combine beans, water and soup base. Cover and let stand overnight at room temperature. The next day, without draining, add ham shanks, onion, celery, half the squash cubes and pepper. Bring to a boil over high heat. Reduce heat to low; cover and simmer for 1-1/2 hours. Remove ham shanks and let cool slightly; remove meat from the bones and chop. Partially mash beans with a potato masher. Add chopped ham and remaining squash cubes to the pot. Simmer, covered, for an additional 20 minutes, or until squash is tender. Add salt and additional pepper if needed. Serves 6 to 8.

Look for colorful old-fashioned cut flowers like zinnias and dwarf sunflowers at farmers' markets or even your neighborhood supermarket. Arrange a generous bunch in a tall stoneware crock for a cheery centerpiece.

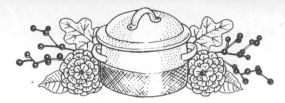

Oh-So-Easy Chili

Donna Jackson
Brandon, MS

Standard football viewing fare at our house in the fall. Add some buttered cornbread and you've got a fantastic meal! The ingredients can also be put in a slow cooker to simmer all day on low.

1 lb. ground beef
1/2 c. onion, chopped
16-oz. can kidney beans
16-oz. can diced tomatoes
8-oz. can tomato sauce

1 T. chili powder
1 t. salt
Optional: shredded Cheddar
   cheese, sour cream

In a large skillet over medium heat, brown beef and onion; drain. Stir in undrained beans and tomatoes, tomato sauce and seasonings. Cover and simmer for 30 minutes, stirring occasionally. Top individual servings with cheese or sour cream, if desired. Serves 4.

Cheesy Beer Corn Muffins

Donna Cash
Pinckney, MI

Wonderful with a bowl of your best chili!

1 c. regular or non-alcoholic beer
3 c. biscuit baking mix
1 c. yellow cornmeal
1 t. baking powder

1 t. cayenne pepper
2 eggs, beaten
1 c. shredded sharp Cheddar
   cheese

Let beer stand until foam settles. In a large bowl, combine biscuit mix, cornmeal, baking powder and cayenne pepper; stir together. Add eggs and beer; mix well. Stir in cheese; spoon into paper-lined muffin cups, filling 2/3 full. Bake at 325 degrees for 12 to 15 minutes, until golden. Makes one dozen.

Fall is sweater weather...hang an old-fashioned peg rack inside the back door so everyone knows just where to find their favorite snuggly sweater!

Soup Supper with
Friends

Slow-Cooked Campfire Stew

Diane Hixon
Niceville, FL

*I used to have a small cafe and one day I made this stew
to serve. It was a big hit...even folks who said they didn't like
corn or butter beans enjoyed it!*

3 potatoes, peeled and diced
1 onion, chopped
2 16-oz. cans stewed tomatoes
16-oz. can butter beans
16-oz. can creamed corn
14-1/2 oz. container shredded
    BBQ beef

14-1/2 oz. container shredded
    BBQ pork
1 T. Worcestershire sauce
1 T. lemon juice
salt and pepper to taste

In a saucepan, cover potatoes and onion with water. Cook over
medium-high heat for 10 to 15 minutes, until tender. Drain, reserving
1/4 cup cooking liquid. Add potatoes, onion and reserved liquid to a
slow cooker along with undrained canned vegetables and remaining
ingredients. Stir well; cover and cook on low setting for 4 hours.
Makes 6 to 8 servings.

Pitch a tent in the backyard on a fall night so the kids can
camp out, tell ghost stories and play flashlight tag.
What a great way to make memories!

Creamy Turkey Soup

Debra Caraballo
Manahawkin, NJ

I started making this soup when I moved to New Jersey from Texas several years ago. It's been a family favorite ever since! I like to add some extra chopped turkey. A roast chicken (or two) can be used also.

1 meaty roast turkey carcass
16 c. water
1 c. butter, sliced
2 onions, peeled and diced
2 stalks celery, thinly sliced

1 c. all-purpose flour
2 carrots, peeled and diced
2 c. half-and-half
1-1/2 c. instant rice, uncooked

In a large stockpot, combine turkey carcass and water. Bring to a boil over high heat; reduce heat to low. Cover and simmer for one hour. Remove carcass from broth and let cool, reserving 12 cups broth for the soup. Cut meat from bones and set aside. Melt butter in a separate soup pot. Add onion and celery; cook over medium heat until tender. Add flour, blending well; add 4 cups reserved broth and simmer until thickened. Meanwhile, add carrots to a small saucepan of boiling water. Cook about 5 minutes, until partially tender; drain. When soup is thickened, stir in remaining broth, half-and-half, carrots, reserved turkey and rice. Simmer for 30 to 35 minutes, stirring occasionally, until rice is cooked. Makes 10 to 12 servings.

Make Jack-o'-Lanterns last longer. Add a tablespoon of bleach to a quart of water, then use a soft cloth to wipe the pumpkin inside & out. Apply a thin layer of petroleum jelly to the cut surfaces.

Mashed Potato & Turkey Soup

Valarie Dennard
Palatka, FL

During the Thanksgiving weekend, after the weeks of planning, shopping and cooking are over, this recipe is my ticket to go shopping, catch a movie or just relax with my family & friends.

2 T. butter
1 yellow onion, diced
2 c. sliced mushrooms
1 carrot, peeled and coarsely
    grated

1 t. dried thyme
4 c. low-sodium chicken broth
3 c. mashed potatoes
2 c. cooked turkey, chopped
salt and pepper to taste

Melt butter in a large saucepan over medium-high heat. Add onion, mushrooms, carrot and thyme. Sauté until onion is translucent, about 4 to 5 minutes. Add broth and mashed potatoes; stir until potatoes are mostly dissolved and broth is smooth. Add turkey; bring to a simmer. Reduce heat to medium-low. Cook, stirring occasionally, until heated through, about 10 minutes. Serves 6.

Fall is the ideal time to plant daffodils, tulips and other spring flowering bulbs! There are lots of varieties to choose from at the neighborhood garden center. Plant bulbs in October when the weather is cool.

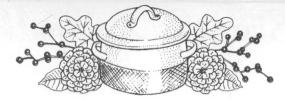

Fiery Tortilla Soup

Lindsey Chrostowski
Janesville, WI

*My family and I enjoy this recipe outside by our campfire on cool
fall nights...it sets such a nice tone for the season!*

1 T. oil
1 yellow pepper, chopped
1 jalapeño pepper, chopped
1 onion, chopped
1 T. ground cumin, or to taste
3 to 4 T. fresh cilantro, chopped
salt and pepper to taste
32-oz. container chicken broth

12-oz. pkg. grilled chicken
  strips, chopped
15-oz. can Mexican-style corn
  with beans
15-oz. can Mexican-style diced
  tomatoes
Garnish: crushed tortilla chips,
  shredded Cheddar cheese

Heat oil in a skillet over medium heat. Sauté peppers and onion until
tender, about 10 minutes. Stir in cumin, cilantro, salt and pepper.
Transfer pepper mixture to a large soup pot. Add broth, chicken and
undrained corn and tomatoes. Simmer over medium heat for about
15 minutes, until heated through. To serve, ladle soup into bowls; top
with crushed tortilla chips and shredded cheese. Serves 4.

Making a campfire? Here are some
quick tips for getting it started and
ready for cooking. Crumple newspaper
for the first layer, then add dry twigs.
Light the paper, add several pieces
of wood and let it burn down to
glowing red coals. Let it burn
down a bit more, then
place the cooking
grate over the coals.

Chicken & Barley Soup

Wendy Henderson
Neodesha, KS

On cold days, I like to put this soup into the slow cooker before I leave for work. When I get home, it's ready to eat with some nice crusty French bread. My daughter and I came up with this easy recipe to use up some leftovers, and it has been a favorite ever since.

1 onion, diced
2 stalks celery, diced
2 carrots, peeled and diced
1 T. olive oil
2 32-oz. containers chicken
   broth

2 c. cooked chicken, diced
1/2 lb. sliced mushrooms
1 t. dried rosemary
1 t. dried oregano
1-1/2 c. quick-cooking barley,
   uncooked

In a skillet over medium heat, sauté onion, celery and carrots in oil until tender; drain. In a slow cooker, combine onion mixture and remaining ingredients; stir. Cover and cook on low setting for 6 to 8 hours, until barley is tender. Serves 6 to 8.

Nothing hits the spot in chilly weather like a bowl of hot soup. Make a double or triple batch of chicken soup, adding only basic veggies and seasonings. Divide into portions and freeze. Noodles, barley and rice can be added when soup is reheated for serving...three kinds of soup with no extra effort!

Mom's Beef Vegetable Soup
Angie Womack
Cave City, AR

After my oldest son got married, he would call and ask me how to make different dishes. When I gave him this recipe, he said, "Mom, this is easy...I always thought you were really working hard when you made this soup!" No more shortcuts for him!

1-1/2 lbs. ground beef
1/2 c. onion, diced
1 clove garlic, minced
2 8-oz. cans tomato sauce
14-1/2 oz. can Italian-style
    diced tomatoes

29-oz. can mixed stew
    vegetables
2 c. water
salt and pepper to taste
Garnish: shredded Cheddar
    cheese

Brown beef in a soup pot over medium heat; drain. Add onion and garlic; cook until tender. Add tomato sauce, undrained tomatoes and mixed vegetables, water and seasonings. Bring to a boil; lower heat and simmer for 30 minutes. More water may be added for a thinner soup. Serve topped with cheese. Serves 8.

Nanny Newman's Chili
Libby Chapman
South Bloomingville, OH

This chili was a staple on all the camping trips my late husband took with his mother and sister, growing up. It's so easy to take the cans and the browned beef and onion in your cooler...almost an instant meal when you arrive at your campsite!

1 to 1-1/2 lbs. lean ground beef
1 onion, chopped
2 16-oz. cans kidney beans
2 15-oz. cans spaghetti

2 10-3/4 oz. cans tomato soup
1 T. ground cumin, or to taste
Garnish: oyster crackers, cheese
    cubes, celery sticks

Brown beef and onion in a large saucepan over medium heat; drain. Add remaining ingredients except garnish; heat through. Garnish as desired. Serves 4 to 6.

Soup Supper with
Friends

Luke's Baggie Bread

Barb Bargdill
Gooseberry Patch

*My eight-year-old nephew Luke made this bread for me for Mothers'
Day, after learning how to do it in school. He made it all by himself
and it was absolutely wonderful...very dense and crusty! His mom
says that this recipe is pretty easy for kids to do all by themselves or
with a little help. If you wish, use 2 cups all-purpose flour and one
cup whole-wheat flour.*

3 c. all-purpose flour, divided
3 T. sugar
1 env. rapid-rise yeast
1 c. warm water

3 T. non-fat dry milk
3 T. olive oil
1-1/2 t. salt

In a large plastic zipping bag, combine one cup flour, sugar and yeast.
Heat water to 110 to 115 degrees and add to bag. Squeeze most of the
air out of the bag and seal. Squish with your hands until well blended.
Set aside at room temperature to rest for 10 minutes, or until bubbles
appear. In a separate bowl, stir together one cup remaining flour,
milk, oil and salt. Pour into bag; squeeze out most of the air. Seal;
squish until well blended. Add remaining flour to bag; continue mixing
until well blended. Remove dough from bag; place on a floured surface.
Knead for 5 to 8 minutes; form into a loaf. Place in a greased
8"x4" loaf pan. Cover with a tea towel. Let rise for about 30 minutes,
or until your finger leaves an impression when you gently poke the
top of the loaf. Bake at 375 degrees for 35 minutes, or until golden.
Makes one loaf.

Stock up on homemade jams, jellies and
preserves at autumn farmers' markets...
you can't have too many! Bake up a
batch of apple butter muffins, spoon
raspberry jam into thumbprint
cookies, glaze baked chicken with
peach preserves...even add a cute
fabric topper to turn a jar of jam
into a last-minute hostess gift.

Portuguese Pea Stew

Monica Amorim
Orland, CA

This slow-cooker recipe is a version of my grandmother's pea stew. It's one of my husband's favorites...he doesn't eat many vegetables, but he loves this soup! The easiest recipe I've ever made. Just toss everything in and when dinnertime rolls around you're all set!

3 boneless, skinless chicken breasts, cut in half
2 15-oz. cans peas
8-oz. can tomato sauce
14-oz. can chicken broth

2 to 4 potatoes, peeled and cubed
1/4 c. dried, minced onion
1 T. garlic, minced
1 T. seasoning salt

Combine all ingredients in a slow cooker; stir. Cover and cook on low setting for 6 to 8 hours, or on high setting for 4 to 6 hours. Serves 6 to 8.

It was my senior year in high school and I had just been crowned Barnwarming Queen at the annual fall Future Farmers of America event. I was sitting on a bale of hay with my boyfriend Jack and our brothers. I asked Jack for a piece of chewing gum, and I was completely surprised when he dropped an engagement ring in my hand instead! We've been married for more than 30 years...and I'm just as crazy about him now as I was on that special evening so long ago. Fall is still my favorite time of year!

–Sonya Jones, West Plains, MO

Soup Supper with Friends

Mémère's Vegetable Soup

Tammi Moore
Durham, ME

I remember when I was a little girl, my great-grandmother would make this soup when we were sick...her soup always seemed to cure anything! She used to send the leftovers home with us packed in a big canning jar.

1 beef soup bone
8 to 10 c. water
salt and pepper to taste
1 lb. carrots, peeled and diced

1/2 head cabbage, diced
1 turnip, peeled and diced
1 to 2 onions, diced
6-oz. can tomato paste

Place soup bone and water in a soup pot; season with salt and pepper. Bring to a boil over high heat. Reduce heat to low; simmer for 45 minutes to one hour. Remove bone; add vegetables to the pot. Cook vegetables until tender. Stir in tomato paste and 2 to 3 tablespoons Salt Herbs. Taste and adjust seasoning if necessary. If soup is too thick, add a little more water. Serves 4 to 6.

Salt Herbs:

1 bunch green onions, thinly
    sliced
1 bunch curly parsley, minced

2 to 3 T. kosher salt

Mix onions and parsley in a bowl; sprinkle with salt. Cover and let stand overnight at room temperature. In the morning, stir again. Transfer mixture to a freezer-safe container. May be kept frozen for several months (will not freeze solid) and used as needed.

Gather bundles of garden-fresh herbs and tie with raffia. To each bundle, add a little tag that you've written a friend's name on. A fragrant gift and a terrific way to use the last of the herbs still growing in your garden.

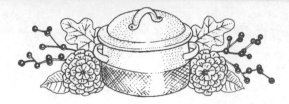

Tangy Salmon Cream Soup

Lisa McClelland
Columbus, OH

I created this recipe for a meal that's quick, yet fancy enough to set before company when unexpected guests come for the evening.

8-oz. pkg. cream cheese, cubed
    and softened
1 c. milk
14-oz. can chicken broth
2-1/2 t. Dijon mustard
1-1/2 t. fresh dill, chopped

1 c. frozen peas
2 green onions, sliced
12-oz. pkg. smoked salmon,
    flaked
Optional: chopped fresh chives

In a saucepan over medium-low heat, combine all ingredients except salmon and chives. Cook, stirring often, until cheese is melted and soup is smooth. Stir in salmon; heat through. Sprinkle with chives, if desired. Makes 4 servings.

A family recipe book is a wonderful way to preserve one generation's traditions for the next. Ask everyone to send copies of their most-requested recipes, just the way they make them. Combine all the recipes into a book and have enough copies made for everyone...a delightful take-home for Thanksgiving dinner.

Soup Supper with
Friends

Karen's Fish Chowder

Ashley Billings
Norfolk, VA

This recipe came from my mother-in-law...it's one of my husband's favorite soups! Serve with hearty bread for a satisfying cool-weather meal.

2 to 3 T. salt pork, diced
1 onion, chopped
2 potatoes, peeled and diced
1 lb. haddock, cut into chunks

12-oz. can evaporated milk
1/4 c. milk
Garnish: 1 T. butter, sliced

In a large saucepan over medium heat, cook salt pork until crisp and golden. Add onion; cook for 3 to 4 minutes. Add potatoes and enough water to cover; bring to a boil. Cook for 5 to 6 minutes; add fish and bring to a boil again. Reduce heat; simmer until fish is done and breaks up easily with a wooden spoon. Stir in milks; top with butter. For the best flavor, make ahead of time, let cool and reheat to serve. Makes 4 servings.

Add old-fashioned flavor to pots of soup, potatoes, green beans and navy beans with a few slices of salt pork. Look for it at the meat counter...if you don't have any, bacon or ham can be substituted.

Dad Cole's Hearty Beef Stew

Bonnie Cole
Easley, SC

Whenever we go to visit my father-in-law in Michigan, he makes us this wonderful stew. It's always associated with good times and laughter. He serves this with his homemade oatmeal rolls.

2 lbs. stew beef, cut into
   1-1/2 inch cubes
6 to 7 potatoes, peeled and cut
   into 1-1/2 inch cubes
8 carrots, peeled and cut into
   1-1/2 inch pieces
4 to 5 stalks celery, cut into
   1-inch pieces
2 onions, cut into wedges

4-oz. can sliced mushrooms,
   drained
1-1/2 t. dried thyme
1 t. sugar
2 bay leaves
1 cube beef bouillon
1-1/2 t. salt
1/3 c. instant tapioca, uncooked
3 c. tomato juice

In a Dutch oven, layer beef and vegetables. Sprinkle with thyme and sugar; tuck in bay leaves and bouillon cube. Add salt to tapioca; sprinkle over all. Drizzle tomato juice over everything. Cover and bake at 300 degrees for 3 hours, stirring occasionally, until beef and vegetables are tender. Discard bay leaves before serving. If made ahead and refrigerated, stew will thicken; add additional tomato juice or water when reheating. Serves 6 to 8.

Serving soup to little eaters? Cut out Jack-o'-Lantern faces
from cheese slices. After spooning soup into bowls,
top servings with the cut-out shapes. How fun!

Homestyle Oatmeal Bread

Janis Parr
Ontario, Canada

This hearty bread is nutritious and delicious too. Since the dough needs to refrigerate overnight before baking, it's a perfect make-ahead for Thanksgiving.

2 envs. active dry yeast
1/2 c. warm water
1-1/4 c. warm milk
1/4 c. brown sugar, packed
1 T. salt
3 T. butter, melted

5 to 6 c. all-purpose flour, divided
1 c. quick-cooking oats, uncooked
1 T. oil

In a large bowl, dissolve yeast in very warm water, 110 to 115 degrees. Stir in milk, brown sugar, salt and butter. Add 2 cups flour and beat for 3 minutes by hand, until smooth. Add one cup flour and all the oats. Beat by hand until smooth, about 150 strokes. Add enough of remaining flour to make a soft dough. Turn dough onto a floured surface. Knead for 8 to 10 minutes, until smooth and elastic. Cover dough with a tea towel; allow to rest for 20 minutes. Divide dough in half. Form into 2 loaves; place each in a greased 8-1/2"x4-1/2" loaf pan. Brush loaves with oil. Cover again; refrigerate loaves overnight. When ready to bake, remove loaves from refrigerator and let stand, uncovered, for 20 minutes at room temperature. Bake at 400 degrees for 35 to 40 minutes, until golden. Immediately turn loaves out of pans; cool on a wire rack. Makes 2 loaves.

Baking yeast bread from scratch? A convenient place to let the dough rise is inside your microwave. Heat a mug of water on high for 2 minutes. Then remove the mug, place the covered bowl of dough inside and close the door.

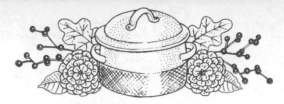

Apple-Walnut Muffins

Michael Curry
Ardmore, OK

Everybody loves these muffins and they go fast! Since I have high cholesterol, I adapted a recipe to use no-calorie sweetener. You can use half sugar and half sweetener, if you prefer.

1-1/2 c. all-purpose flour
1 c. sugar or low-calorie
  powdered sweetener
  blend for baking
1 t. baking powder
1 t. baking soda
1/2 t. salt
1-1/2 t. apple pie spice

2 c. apples, peeled, cored and
  chopped
1 c. chopped walnuts
1 c. water
1/3 c. canola oil
1 T. cider vinegar
1 t. vanilla extract

In a large bowl, sift together flour, sugar or sweetener, baking powder, baking soda, salt and spice. Stir in apples and walnuts. Add remaining ingredients; mix until moistened. Pour batter into a greased muffin tin, filling cups 2/3 full. Bake at 350 degrees for about 30 minutes. Makes about one dozen.

Patterned pumpkin centerpieces in no time! Stencil a favorite pattern on a white Lumina pumpkin or paint rings of white latex paint around a pale orange pumpkin to resemble a yellowware bowl.

Soup Supper with Friends

Parmesan Potato Soup

Trisha Donley
Pinedale, WY

Use freshly grated Parmesan cheese if you can...it adds terrific flavor to this heartwarming soup.

4 baking potatoes
3/4 c. onion, chopped
1/2 c. butter
1/2 c. all-purpose flour
salt and pepper to taste

4-1/2 c. chicken broth
6 c. milk
1 c. shredded Parmesan cheese
10 slices bacon, crisply cooked
   and crumbled

Pierce potatoes several times with a fork. Bake in an oven or cook in microwave until tender. Peel and cube potatoes when cool; set aside. In a large soup kettle over medium heat, sauté onion in butter until tender. Stir in flour, salt and pepper. Gradually add broth, stirring constantly; bring to a boil. Cook and stir for 2 to 3 minutes. Add potatoes; return to a boil. Reduce heat to low; cover and simmer for 10 minutes. Stir in milk, cheese and bacon just before serving. Makes 10 to 12 servings.

Welcome autumn with a new wreath on the front door! Decorate a purchased wreath form with clusters of seed pods, nuts, fallen leaves, ornamental grasses and other fall finds...a terrific way to enjoy items collected on a leaf-peeping walk! Simply attach the fall finds with wire, florist pins or hot glue.

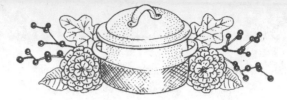

Chourico & Kale Soup

Jan Walsh
Plymouth, MA

During New England winters, we hardy folks are always looking for a stick-to-your-ribs soup. Especially good on a snowy night...easy to reheat after work! Serve with crusty ciabatta bread.

1-lb. Portuguese chourico pork
   sausage link
8 c. water
4 to 6 potatoes, peeled and
   chopped
4 to 6 carrots, peeled and
   chopped
2 to 3 onions, peeled and sliced
3 to 4 cloves garlic, peeled and
   chopped

1/4 c. olive oil
14-oz. can chicken broth
1/8 t. salt
1/4 t. pepper
1/8 t. nutmeg
1 to 2 lbs. kale, trimmed
   and torn
Garnish: additional olive oil,
   grated Parmesan cheese

Place sausage and water in a soup pot over medium-high heat. Boil for 45 minutes. Remove sausage, reserving liquid in saucepan; slice sausage on an angle and set aside. Add potatoes and carrots to reserved liquid. Cook over medium heat for 20 minutes. Meanwhile, in a separate skillet over medium heat, sauté onions and garlic in olive oil for several minutes. Add sliced sausage; cook just until onions are golden. Add sausage mixture and remaining ingredients except garnish to soup pot. Simmer over medium-low heat for 30 minutes, until kale is wilted. At serving time, drizzle each bowl of soup with olive oil; sprinkle with Parmesan cheese. Makes 14 to 16 servings.

Twisty bread sticks are a tasty go-with for soup. Brush refrigerated bread stick dough with a little beaten egg. Dust with Italian seasoning and garlic powder, then pop in the oven until golden and toasty. Yummy!

Creamy Corn Bisque

Sharon Mason
Sylvania, OH

This goes together in a jiffy on a weeknight and reheats well.

1/4 c. butter
1 onion, chopped
1/4 c. all-purpose flour
1/2 t. salt
1/8 t. pepper
4 c. milk
15-1/4 oz. can corn, drained

1 lb. smoked pork sausage, diced
2 c. potatoes, cooked, peeled and cubed
Garnish: shredded Cheddar cheese

Melt butter in a large saucepan over medium heat. Add onion; cook and stir until tender. Add flour, salt and pepper; cook, stirring constantly, for one minute. Add milk. Increase heat to medium-high and bring to a boil, stirring constantly. Boil and stir for one minute. Add corn and sausage; return to a boil. Reduce heat to medium-low and simmer for 10 minutes. Stir in potatoes; heat through. Top each serving with shredded cheese. Serves 8.

Invite everyone to a soup & sandwich party...perfect for game day! With a big pot of your heartiest soup or chili simmering on the stove, freshly made grilled cheese sandwiches and brownies for dessert, you'll all have time to relax and enjoy the game.

My Best Bean & Bacon Soup

Carol Delozier
East Freedom, PA

I've always loved the flavor of navy beans with ham or bacon. The Pennsylvania Dutch-style rivels are fun and easy to make. Enjoy!

1 lb. bacon, cut into 1-inch
   pieces
2 15-1/2 oz. cans Great
   Northern beans

4 c. water
salt to taste
3 eggs, beaten
3/4 to 1 c. all-purpose flour

In a skillet over medium heat, cook bacon to desired crispness; drain and set aside. Pour undrained beans into a large saucepan; stir in water, bacon and salt to taste. Simmer over medium heat for 30 minutes, stirring often. To make rivels, mix eggs with enough flour to make a slightly thickened batter. Drop batter by spoonfuls into boiling broth. Cover and cook about 15 to 20 minutes longer. Makes 6 servings.

Back-to-school time isn't just for kids. Treat yourself to a craft class like crocheting, jewelry making or scrapbooking that you've been longing to try...take a girlfriend along with you!

Cowpoke Cornbread

Jana Wilson
Laramie, WY

I used to do all the baking for Deerwood Ranch, our family-owned guest ranch. I would make this sweet cornbread for the Thursday night camp-out meals...it was a favorite of many guests.

3 c. all-purpose flour
1 c. cornmeal
1-1/3 c. sugar
2 T. baking powder
1 t. salt

2-1/2 c. milk
2/3 c. canola oil
4 eggs, beaten
6 T. butter, melted

Mix flour, cornmeal, sugar, baking powder and salt in a large bowl. Whisk together milk, oil and eggs in a separate bowl. Add milk mixture to flour mixture; stir until blended. Add butter and stir until incorporated. Pour batter into a lightly greased 13"x9" baking pan. Bake at 350 degrees for about 35 minutes, or until golden. Cut into squares. Makes 18 to 20 servings.

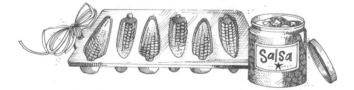

When I was a child we rented from my grandparents; who farmed the land. At corn-picking time, lunch would be set up in our yard on plywood boards set on sawhorses. Mom and Grandma would make ham or chicken sandwiches, hot and cold potato salad, gelatin salad with strawberries and pineapple, made-from-scratch chocolate cake with peanut butter frosting and all kinds of pickles that they had put up from the garden. Although my grandparents and Mom are gone now, I still put up the same pickles, make the same cake and frosting and carry water to the garden for my husband. I'm glad I have all these good memories!

–Anna Ertl, Franksville, WI

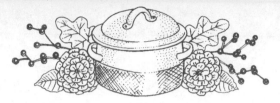

Italian Sausage-Zucchini Soup

Nancy Dancisin
Butler, PA

I got this recipe from my best friend's Italian grandmother more than 30 years ago. I've made a few changes over the years, and it's still one of my family's favorites. This is also good made in a slow cooker...cook on the low setting for 6 to 8 hours.

1 lb. ground pork sausage
1 onion, chopped
2 cloves garlic, chopped
3 green peppers, chopped
10-3/4 oz. can tomato soup
1-1/4 c. water
32-oz. can crushed tomatoes

2 zucchini, peeled and diced
salt and pepper to taste
3 T. dried parsley
2 t. dried oregano
2 t. dried basil
Garnish: shredded or sliced
provolone cheese

In a large soup pot over medium heat, sauté sausage with onion, garlic and green peppers until sausage is browned and vegetables are softened. Drain; add soup, water, tomatoes and zucchini. Season with salt and pepper; add herbs. Reduce heat to low. Simmer soup, uncovered, for 2 to 3 hours, adding more water if needed. Serve with shredded cheese or a slice of cheese to melt on top. Serves 6 to 8.

Gather the last of the garden veggies to freeze and enjoy throughout the winter. Slice or cube carrots, onions, corn, squash and tomatoes. Combine them in gallon-size plastic zipping bags...flavorful stews and soups will be ready in no time!

Chicken Enchilada Soup

Patti Wafford
Mount Vernon, TX

This is my son's favorite soup...and it's so simple to make! I process the green chiles in the blender with some of the broth because he loves the flavor of the chiles, but not the texture.

3 14-oz. cans chicken broth
3 10-3/4 oz. cans cream of
   chicken soup
4-oz. can chopped mild green
   chiles

2 c. cooked chicken, diced
1/2 t. chili powder
16-oz. pkg. pasteurized process
   cheese spread, cubed
Garnish: tortilla chips

In a stockpot, mix all ingredients except cheese and garnish. Cook over medium heat until smooth, about 10 to 15 minutes, stirring occasionally. Reduce heat to low; add cheese. Simmer without boiling until cheese has melted; keep stirring to prevent sticking to bottom of pan. To serve, line soup bowls with tortilla chips; ladle soup over chips. Serves 6 to 8.

Crunchy tortilla strips are a tasty addition to southwestern-style soups. Cut corn tortillas into thin strips, then deep-fry quickly. Drain on paper towels before sprinkling over bowls of soup. Try red or blue tortilla chips just for fun!

Pork Stew & Dumplin's

Constance Shortel
Orlando, FL

It doesn't get really cold here in Florida very often, but when it does, this is one of my favorite meals to make. It makes good use of the rosemary bush growing in our backyard.

1 lb. boneless pork chops, cubed
1 onion, chopped
2 T. butter
4 14-oz. cans chicken broth
2 potatoes, peeled and cubed
1/2 c. celery, chopped
1 c. corn

1-1/2 t. dried rosemary
1 t. garlic powder
10-oz. pkg. favorite frozen
  vegetables
1/4 c. all-purpose flour
1 c. water

In a large soup pot over medium-high heat, brown pork and onion in butter. Add remaining ingredients except frozen vegetables, flour and water; bring to a boil. Reduce heat to low; cover and simmer 45 minutes, until potatoes are tender and pork is no longer pink. Add frozen vegetables. In a small bowl, whisk together flour and water; stir into stew. Continue to simmer while preparing Rosemary Dumplin's. Drop dumpling batter by tablespoonfuls into hot stew. Simmer, uncovered, 25 additional minutes, or until dumplings are fluffy and no longer doughy. Serves 6 to 8.

Rosemary Dumplin's:

1-1/2 c. all-purpose flour
1 T. sugar
2 t. baking powder
1/2 t. salt

2 t. dried rosemary
2/3 c. milk
1 egg, lightly beaten
2 T. oil

In a bowl, stir all ingredients together.

To get the most flavor from dried herbs, crumble them
in your hand before adding to a dish.

Hungarian Beef Soup

Phyllis Wessling
Garner, IA

We love soup! This one is a favorite when we have soup supper gatherings. It's easy to prepare, and leftovers are wonderful for next-day lunches at work. Serve with a basket of hearty rye bread.

2 to 4 T. oil
3 lbs. lean stew beef, cubed
  and divided
2 T. butter
2 onions, chopped
1 clove garlic, pressed
5 c. water
2 tomatoes, coarsely chopped
1 T. paprika, or to taste

1 t. red pepper flakes, or to taste
1 t. caraway seed
2 t. salt, or to taste
1/8 t. white pepper
3 to 4 potatoes, peeled and
  cubed
1 red pepper, cut into strips
Optional: sour cream, sliced
  avocado

Heat 2 tablespoons oil in a Dutch oven over medium-high heat. Add 1/4 of the beef cubes and cook until browned; remove to a bowl. Brown remaining beef in batches, adding more oil as necessary. When all the beef is well-browned, discard pan drippings. Melt butter in the same pan over medium heat. Cook onions and garlic until soft and golden. Return beef cubes to pan; stir in water, tomatoes and seasonings. Bring to a boil. Reduce heat to low; cover and simmer about 2-1/2 hours, until beef is tender. Add potatoes and red pepper; simmer another 30 minutes, or until tender. Season with more salt before serving, if necessary. Garnish as desired and serve. Soup may also be prepared a day ahead. Simmer until beef is tender; cover and refrigerate several hours to overnight. Before serving, skim off any fat. Bring soup to a simmer; add potatoes and continue cooking until tender. Makes 6 to 8 servings.

Drop unpeeled cloves of garlic into a cup of cold water for a few minutes...the garlic will pop right out of its skin.

Pumpkin Spice Muffins

Ruth Thompson
Dublin, NH

We live near Keene, New Hampshire, the first town in the USA to hold the record for the most pumpkins lit at one time! A few years ago I helped bake muffins to sell at the pumpkin festival as a church fundraiser. We sold out that night...they're scrumptious!

18-1/4 oz. pkg. spice cake mix
15-oz. can pumpkin
3 eggs, beaten

1/3 c. oil
1/3 c. water

In a bowl, beat all ingredients together. Pour batter into greased or paper-lined muffin cups, filling 2/3 full. Bake at 350 degrees for 20 minutes, or until golden. Makes 2 dozen.

Cranberry-Pumpkin Muffins

Nancy Girard
Chesapeake, VA

These muffins combine the best fall flavors...yum!

1 c. canned pumpkin
2 eggs, lightly beaten
2 c. sugar
1/2 c. canola oil
2-1/4 c. all-purpose flour

1 T. pumpkin pie spice
1 t. baking soda
1/2 t. salt
1 c. fresh or frozen cranberries,
   chopped

In a bowl, combine pumpkin, eggs, sugar and oil; mix well. In a separate large bowl, combine flour, spice, baking soda and salt. Make a well in the center of flour mixture; pour pumpkin mixture into well. Stir just until dry ingredients are moistened. Stir in cranberries (no need to thaw if frozen). Spoon into greased or paper-lined muffin cups, filling 2/3 full. Bake at 350 degrees for about 20 to 30 minutes, testing with a toothpick for doneness after 20 minutes. Makes one dozen.

A baker's secret! Grease muffin cups on the bottoms and just halfway up the sides...muffins will bake up nicely puffed on top.

Soup Supper with
Friends

Feel-Better Chicken Soup

Yvette Garza
Livingston, CA

*I make a big batch of this soup around flu season and take it
to friends who are feeling under the weather. It's just what
the doctor ordered!*

3 lbs. chicken thighs and legs	6 carrots, peeled and chopped
salt and pepper to taste	6 stalks celery, chopped
1/2 c. oil	1 onion, chopped
16 c. water	2 T. fresh parsley, chopped
9 T. chicken bouillon granules	2 t. dried thyme
3 cloves garlic, pressed	2 c. long-cooking rice, uncooked

Season chicken with salt and pepper; set aside. In a large skillet, heat
oil over medium-high heat. Cook chicken for about 8 minutes on each
side, until browned. Meanwhile, in a soup pot, bring water and
bouillon to a boil over medium-high heat. Reduce to a simmer; add
browned chicken and garlic. Simmer for about 20 minutes. Remove
soup pot from heat. Remove chicken to a platter; let cool. Pull apart
chicken, discarding skin and bones. Skim fat from broth; return soup
pot to high heat. Stir in chicken, vegetables and herbs. Reduce to a
simmer; stir in rice. Cover and simmer for about 20 to 30 minutes,
until rice is cooked. Add more salt and pepper, if needed. Serves 16.

A friend who's under the weather would love a goodie basket
delivered to her door. Fill it with homemade soup and bread, a
good book and a pair of fuzzy socks. Just right for beating a cold!

Kitchen Cupboard Soup

Angela Gojmerac
Monterey, TN

A quick & easy recipe for days when the wind is howling outside your windows! The veggies and broth can be changed to use what you have on hand. Serve with crusty bread.

1 lb. ground beef
2 T. olive oil
1 clove garlic, chopped
15-oz. can seasoned diced
   tomatoes
15-oz. can green, lima or kidney
   beans
1/2 c. frozen corn
1/2 c. frozen spinach, thawed
32-oz. container chicken, beef or
   vegetable broth
salt and pepper to taste
1/2 c. small shell macaroni,
   uncooked
Garnish: shredded Cheddar
   cheese

In a large saucepan over medium heat, brown beef in oil; drain. Add garlic; cook just until golden. Add undrained tomatoes, undrained beans and remaining ingredients except macaroni and garnish. Bring to a boil. Reduce heat to low; cover and simmer at least 30 minutes. If more liquid is needed, add some water or more broth. Stir in macaroni; cook just until tender, about 10 minutes. Serve in bowls with a sprinkle of shredded cheese. Serves 4.

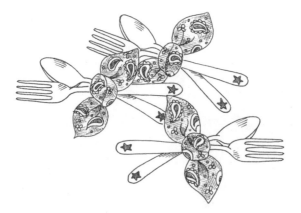

Give tonight's table a little flair...knot a cheery bandanna around each set of flatware. Bandannas come in so many bright colors, everyone can choose their own favorite.

Savory Onion & Garlic Soup
Judy Olson
Alberta, Canada

*This soup is awesome served with a nice thick slice
of homemade whole-wheat bread.*

2 T. olive oil
1 sweet onion, chopped
1 leek, white part only, diced
8 c. vegetable broth
2 potatoes, peeled and cubed

15 cloves garlic, peeled
1 c. half-and-half
salt and pepper to taste
Garnish: snipped fresh chives

Heat oil in a Dutch oven over medium heat. Add onion and leek; cook and stir until tender, about 5 minutes. Add broth and bring to a boil; stir in potatoes and garlic. Reduce heat to low; cover and simmer for one hour. In a food processor, working in batches as necessary, combine soup and half-and-half; process until smooth. Return soup to Dutch oven and heat through. Add salt and pepper to taste. Garnish with chives. Serves 6.

By all these lovely tokens
September days are here,
With summer's best of weather
And autumn's best of cheer.

–Helen Hunt Jackson

Satisfying Slim-Down Soup

Beckie Apple
Grannis, AR

My friends and I have enjoyed this recipe for many years and it is especially popular right after the holidays! It's very tasty, low-calorie, low-cost and makes enough to last several days.

4 c. hot water
1.35-oz. pkg. onion soup mix
1/4 t. garlic powder
1/4 t. salt
1/4 t. pepper
1 head cabbage, thinly sliced

1 onion, coarsely chopped
4 stalks celery, sliced
2 carrots, peeled and sliced
3 T. bacon bits
3 15-oz. cans seasoned or plain
   diced tomatoes

Combine hot water, soup mix and seasonings in a soup pot; mix well. Stir in cabbage, onion, celery and carrots; simmer over medium heat for 20 minutes. Stir in bacon bits and undrained tomatoes; continue cooking over low heat for 20 minutes. Makes 10 to 12 servings.

Visit a pottery studio with friends and try your hand at throwing clay soup bowls. Decorate and fire your creations to take home...even the simplest bowls will serve up fun memories along with the soup!

Simple Harvest Supper

Sausage & Apple Kraut

Sheryl Eastman
Wixom, MI

I learned how to make this dish a long time ago and still enjoy it.
Serve with mashed potatoes, buttered green beans and fresh-baked
rolls for a satisfying chilly-weather meal.

27-oz. jar sauerkraut, drained,
  rinsed and divided
14-oz. smoked or Kielbasa
  sausage ring, sliced and
  divided
2 tart apples, peeled, cored
  and diced

1/2 c. brown sugar, packed
  and divided
2 c. apple cider or apple juice,
  divided

In a lightly greased 13"x9" baking pan, layer half of sauerkraut, half
of sausage and all the apples. Sprinkle with 1/4 cup brown sugar.
Pour one cup cider or juice over top. Repeat layering with remaining
sauerkraut, sausage, brown sugar and cider or juice. Cover and bake at
350 degrees for 1-1/2 hours, or until sauerkraut is caramelized and
golden. Serves 4 to 6.

September always reminds me of canning with my mom. My dad
worked really hard to grow the best garden around. Mom and I
canned everything from our garden...fresh green beans, tomatoes
and lots of potatoes. I really miss those days of canning with my
mom and the fresh foods from the garden now that both my
parents are gone. But my adult son Greg decided to grow a
garden...it turned out really well for his first one! Now he is
canning green beans and carrots and I told him I want to come
help. So now I will have new memories with him and we can
reminisce about his papa's garden. Memories are great!

–Laura Naegle, Enumclaw, WA

Simple Harvest
Supper

Roasted Chicken Sausage & Potatoes

Emily Pselos
Temecula, CA

I got this recipe several years ago. It's quick and very good...my husband loves it! I buy the chicken sausage from a local market that makes their own. Different flavors of sausage may be used and different fresh or dried herbs work well too. If I am using some nice, thick sausage links, I halve them after 15 minutes, once they've firmed up a bit, so they finish cooking faster.

1-1/2 lbs. smoked chicken
    sausage links
1-1/2 lbs. russet potatoes,
    peeled and cubed

2 T. olive oil
1 T. fresh rosemary, chopped,
    or 1 t. dried rosemary
coarse salt and pepper to taste

Pierce sausage links all over with a fork; place on a rimmed baking sheet with potatoes. Drizzle with olive oil; sprinkle with rosemary and season generously with salt and pepper. Toss to coat; spread in an even layer. Bake, uncovered, at 450 degrees for 30 to 35 minutes, stirring occasionally, until sausage links are golden and potatoes are tender. If desired, cut sausage links in half crosswise before serving. Serves 4.

On busy fall weekends when you're getting together with friends, a simple make-ahead casserole is perfect. Assemble it the day before and refrigerate, then pop it in the oven when you return from barn sale-ing, leaf peeping or getting an early start on holiday shopping.

Grilled Lemon Turkey

Jenny Bishoff
Mountain Lake Park, MD

This is a recipe our whole family enjoys. I put everything together in the morning. When I get home from work, I steam some veggies, slice some bread and toss the turkey on the grill!

1/4 c. olive oil
1/4 c. lemon juice
1/4 c. water
1 T. fresh rosemary, chopped,
    or 1 t. dried rosemary

1 to 2 t. lemon pepper seasoning
1 t. chicken bouillon granules
4 to 6 turkey cutlets

In a one-gallon plastic zipping bag, mix all ingredients except turkey; squeeze bag to mix. Add turkey to bag; seal. Refrigerate 4 hours to overnight, turning occasionally. Drain, discarding marinade. Grill turkey over medium heat about 10 to 15 minutes, turning once, until juices run clear. Serves 4 to 6.

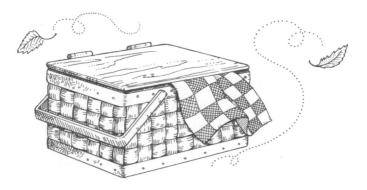

On a beautiful fall day, have a harvest feast outdoors.
Set up a table under the trees, or turn it into a barn party.
Layer woolen blankets on the table, then mix & match
painted chairs for seating. Make dinner fun!

Simple Harvest
Supper

Grilled Sweet Potato Fries

Sara Smith
Crestwood, KY

These fries are scrumptious! A lightning-fast recipe for those warm Indian Summer days...why heat up the kitchen?

3 sweet potatoes, peeled and cut
   into wedges

Optional: 1 t. cinnamon,
   1 T. sugar

Put sweet potato wedges in a microwave-safe dish and cook for 4 minutes on high. Spray wedges with non-stick olive oil spray. Grill wedges over hot coals or medium-high heat for 12 to 15 minutes, turning often, until crisp. If desired, mix cinnamon and sugar in a small bowl. To serve, dip fries into Smoked Honey, then into cinnamon-sugar, if using. Makes 4 servings.

Smoked Honey:

1/2 t. smoke-flavored cooking
   sauce

3 T. honey

Stir ingredients together in a small bowl.

Bring out Mom's vintage Thanksgiving china early to get into the mood for fall. Use the bowls for soup suppers, the teacups for dessert get-togethers and even layer sandwich fixin's on the turkey platter!

Tasty Turkey Roll-Ups

Nancy Marti
Edwardsville, IL

A family favorite that's ready to serve in a jiffy! It's at the top of the request list whenever I ask for dinner suggestions. Serve with a side of steamed vegetables for a delicious meal.

6-oz. pkg. sage-flavored stuffing
   mix
6 to 8 thin slices deli roast
   turkey

12-oz. jar turkey gravy

Prepare stuffing mix according to package directions. Take one slice of turkey and put 2 tablespoons of stuffing on one end. Roll up turkey slice, beginning at the end with the stuffing; secure with a toothpick. Continue until all turkey slices are filled and rolled. Place rolls in a lightly greased 8"x8" baking pan, seam-side down. Spread any extra stuffing around rolls; top with gravy. Bake, uncovered, at 350 degrees for 20 to 30 minutes, until heated through. Makes 4 to 6 servings.

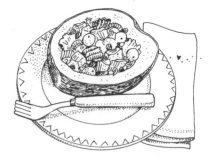

Acorn squash is a fall treat. To prepare it quickly, place squash halves cut-side up in a microwave-safe dish. Top squash with a spoonful of brown sugar, honey or maple syrup. Add a little water to the dish, cover with plastic wrap and microwave on high for 12 to 14 minutes, until squash is very tender.

Simple Harvest
Supper

Easy Ranch Potatoes

Jennie Gist
Gooseberry Patch

*These crispy potato puffs are scrumptious and oh-so easy to fix
for a busy-night supper. Serve them alongside burgers,
hot dogs or baked chicken.*

1/4 c. olive oil
2 .4-oz. pkgs. ranch salad
   dressing mix

32-oz. pkg. frozen potato puffs,
   thawed

In a large bowl, combine oil and salad dressing mix; stir well. Add
potato puffs and toss to coat. Arrange potatoes in a single layer on an
ungreased 15"x10" jelly-roll pan. Bake, uncovered, at 450 degrees for
30 to 35 minutes, stirring every 10 minutes, until potatoes are crisp
and golden. Makes 6 to 8 servings.

Whip up some handy back-to-school clipboards to show off the
children's best artwork, bragging-rights school papers and other
special items. Decorate dollar-store clipboards with paint, add
each child's name with wooden game tiles and hang up the
clipboards on nails...it's that simple.

Grandma's Spaghetti Supreme
Pamela Elkin
Asheville, NC

My mother was given this delicious recipe by her mother, my wonderful Nanny. Mother has made it for us for years. Now it is a big favorite with her four grandsons and we're passing it down to their wives and girlfriends too. It's terrific for covered-dish dinners.

16-oz. pkg. spaghetti, uncooked
1 lb. ground beef or turkey
1/4 c. onion, chopped
2 10-3/4 oz. cans tomato soup

10-3/4 oz. can cream of
  mushroom soup
1-1/2 c. shredded Cheddar
  cheese

Cook spaghetti according to package directions; drain. Meanwhile, in a large skillet over medium heat, brown meat and onion; drain. Add tomato soup and spaghetti; mix together. Transfer to a greased 13"x9" baking pan. Spoon mushroom soup over the top; sprinkle with cheese. Bake, uncovered, at 350 degrees for about 45 minutes, until bubbly around the edges and cheese is melted. Serves 8 to 10.

Make a tabletop Halloween tree! Choose a branch from the backyard. Spray-paint it black, if you like, and stand it securely in a weighted vase. Wind with twinkling orange or purple lights...trim with spooky black crows, tiny ghosts made of white hankies and mini Jack-o'-Lanterns. Boo!

Simple Harvest Supper

Halloween Hash

Suzy Mechling
Round Rock, TX

Mom always made this simple skillet dinner for us in the fall. I have two sisters born on the 28th and 30th of October, and my husband's birthday is on October 31st, so Halloween is a special holiday for us.

1 lb. ground beef
1 onion, chopped
28-oz. can diced tomatoes

15-oz. can kidney beans
10-oz. pkg. frozen corn

In a large skillet over medium heat, brown beef and onion; drain. Stir in undrained tomatoes, beans and corn. Reduce heat to low. Cover and simmer for one hour, stirring occasionally. Serves 6.

My sweetest autumn memories are of Halloween, when our entire family always got together for a reunion at my Aunt Sara Lee & Uncle Sam's home. There would be the most amazing desserts and side dishes you ever tasted, along with apple cider and sweet tea. We would roast wieners and marshmallows on branches whittled to a sharp point. After the hugs, fellowship and full bellies, Uncle Sam would bring out the biggest hay-filled trailer pulled by his old tractor. We'd climb on and he would drive us up & down the old dirt roads, taking us through the woods where ghosts and goblins (our cousins!) would scare us. We would sing and laugh together. When he brought us back, we'd beg for another ride before going home. Some of the people in these precious memories are no longer with us, but the memories will stay with me forever.

–Ben Gothard, Jemison, AL

Oh-So-Good Crispy Chicken
Betty Lou Wright
Hendersonville, TN

I fix this chicken once a week. Not only is it easy to prepare, it fills the house with a wonderful aroma of garlic and cheese. Leftovers are delicious cubed and served on salad greens. Very, very good!

1/4 c. margarine
1/4 t. garlic powder
1/4 c. grated Parmesan cheese
4 boneless, skinless chicken
    breasts

1/2 c. Italian-flavored dry bread
    crumbs

Melt margarine in a small saucepan over low heat. Stir in garlic powder and Parmesan cheese. Dip chicken in margarine mixture; arrange in an ungreased 9"x9" baking pan. Sprinkle bread crumbs on top. Bake, uncovered, at 350 degrees for one to 1-1/2 hours, until golden and chicken juices run clear when pierced. Makes 4 servings.

Honey-Garlic Drumsticks
Gail Blain Prather
Hastings, NE

This recipe is budget-friendly and super-easy...but you'll fix it because it's delicious! A great weeknight staple. I usually enjoy it with steamy, buttered baked potatoes and a crisp tossed salad.

12 chicken drumsticks
1/2 t. salt
1/4 t. pepper

1 c. honey
1 T. hot pepper sauce
1 t. garlic, chopped

Place drumsticks on a rimmed baking sheet; season with salt and pepper. Bake, uncovered, at 400 degrees for 30 minutes. In a bowl, combine remaining ingredients; mix well. Remove drumsticks from oven; brush with honey mixture. Bake for an additional 20 to 25 minutes, until chicken juices run clear. Serves 6 to 8.

Roll up homespun napkins, tie with ribbon bows and slip
a sprig of fresh rosemary under the ribbons...simple!

Simple Harvest
Supper

Buttery Cabbage & Noodles

Andrea Ritter
Slatington, PA

In the region of Pennsylvania where I live, cabbage & noodles is a staple at church functions, flea markets and craft shows. I decided to try my hand at it and came up with this easy recipe. Now I am asked to make it for family gatherings and holidays.

1 yellow onion, chopped
1/4 c. plus 1 to 2 T. butter,
   divided
1 head cabbage, chopped

16-oz. pkg. wide egg noodles or
   bowtie pasta, uncooked
garlic powder, salt and pepper
   to taste

In a stockpot over medium heat, sauté onion in 1/4 cup butter until translucent. Add cabbage; stir until onion and cabbage are well mixed. Cover; simmer over low heat for 45 minutes to an hour, stirring occasionally. Cabbage will cook down. Meanwhile, cook noodles or pasta according to package directions; drain. When cabbage is done cooking, add seasonings to taste. Fold noodles or pasta into cabbage mixture; stir in remaining butter. Cook over low heat until butter is melted. Makes 8 to 10 servings.

Sometimes the simplest front door decorations are the prettiest!
Gather five or six brightly colored ears of Indian corn
by the dried husks and tie with a big ribbon bow.

Sofie's Upside-Down Hamburger Pie

Naomi Costales
Placitas, NM

This recipe was given to me by my mother-in-law. She received it from her own mother-in-law, who was called Grandma Sofie. I never got to meet Sofie, but I treasure this recipe...I love that it cooks in a cast-iron skillet! It is one of my husband's favorites and so easy to make.

1 lb. lean ground beef
1/2 onion, chopped
8-oz. can tomato sauce

salt and pepper to taste
Optional: 1 t. sugar
2 8-1/2 oz. pkgs. cornbread mix

Brown beef and onion in a cast-iron skillet over medium heat; drain. Stir in tomato sauce, salt and pepper. If a sweeter tomato sauce is desired, add sugar. Spread mixture evenly in skillet or transfer to a lightly greased 8"x8" baking pan. Prepare cornbread mix according to package directions. Pour batter evenly over beef, spreading it out to the edges. Bake, uncovered, at 350 degrees for about 30 minutes, until cornbread is set and golden. To serve, invert onto a platter. Serves 4.

A vintage-style oilcloth tablecloth with colorful fruit and flowers adds cheer to any dinner table. Its wipe-clean ease makes it oh-so practical for family meals.

Simple Harvest
Supper

Cheeseburger Macaroni

Shannon Reents
Loudonville, OH

This quick & easy recipe was given to me years ago by a very dear friend. My family still asks for it when they come home!

1 lb. ground beef	1 c. elbow macaroni, uncooked
1 c. onion, chopped	1-1/2 c. shredded Cheddar
14-1/2 oz. can stewed tomatoes	cheese
1 c. water	

Brown beef and onion in a skillet over medium heat; drain. Add undrained tomatoes and water; bring to a boil. Stir in uncooked macaroni. Simmer, uncovered, for 10 minutes, or until macaroni is tender. Remove from heat. Stir in cheese; let stand a few minutes, until cheese melts. Serves 4.

Indian Summer is perfect for a neighborhood block party...the weather is still warm and fall foliage is gorgeous. Set up tables with hay bales to sit on. Everyone can snack on favorite finger foods while waiting for burgers and hot dogs to grill. Don't forget a game of beanbag toss for the kids!

Creamy Skillet Corn

Nola Coons
Gooseberry Patch

This corn dish looks extra special...it's my secret that it's easy!

2 T. olive oil
10-oz. pkg. frozen corn, thawed
1 t. garlic, chopped
1 c. whipping cream

1/2 c. red pepper, diced
1/2 c. green onions, chopped
salt and pepper to taste

Heat oil in a skillet over medium-high heat. Add corn and garlic; cook for 3 minutes. Stir in cream, red pepper and onions; cook until slightly thickened. Season with salt and pepper. Makes 4 servings.

Herb-Buttered Broccoli

Regina Wickline
Pebble Beach, CA

My family just loves fresh broccoli when it's fixed this way!

1/2 c. butter, melted
1/4 c. lemon juice
1 clove garlic, minced

1/4 t. dried oregano
salt and pepper to taste
3 lbs. broccoli, cut into flowerets

In a small bowl, stir together all ingredients except broccoli; set aside. In a large saucepan over medium-high heat, bring one inch of water to a boil. Add broccoli; reduce heat to medium. Cover and cook for 5 to 10 minutes, to desired tenderness. Drain broccoli well and transfer to a serving bowl. Drizzle butter mixture over broccoli. Serves 6.

A quick fall craft...hot-glue large acorn caps onto round magnets for whimsical fridge magnets.

Simple Harvest
Supper

Garlicky Broccoli & Pasta

Heidi Armbruster
Waterford, PA

A delicious side or meatless main dish! We really like garlic, so I use twice as much. If I have leftover plain pasta and/or broccoli on hand, I will toss this dish together after sautéing the garlic.

16-oz. pkg. linguine, rotini or
  other pasta, uncooked
16-oz. pkg. frozen broccoli cuts
1/2 to 3/4 c. margarine

3 to 4 cloves garlic, chopped
salt and pepper to taste
Optional: grated Parmesan
  cheese

If linguine is used, break it up into thirds. Cook pasta according to package directions, adding broccoli to pasta pan; drain and set aside. Melt margarine in the same pan; add garlic and sauté. Return pasta mixture to pan; heat through. Sprinkle with salt and pepper; add Parmesan cheese, if desired. Makes 6 to 8 servings.

Make a warm batch of crostini for dinner...it's easy! Slice a loaf of French bread into one-inch diagonal slices. Melt together 1/2 cup butter with 1/2 cup olive oil and brush over one side of each bread slice. Place oiled-side up on a baking sheet and bake at 300 degrees for 20 to 30 minutes, until toasty.

Macaroni Cheese Twists

Vicki Lanzendorf
Madison, WI

My mom used to make this dish when we were kids, and now I make it for my own kids. Using common pantry ingredients, it is super quick... a terrific meatless weeknight meal paired with a tossed salad and garlic bread.

16-oz. pkg. rotini pasta,
 uncooked
1/2 c. green pepper, diced
1 clove garlic, minced
1 c. onion, chopped
1 T. olive oil
2 8-oz. cans tomato sauce

1 c. water
2 T. fresh parsley, chopped
1/2 t. dried oregano
1/4 lb. pasteurized process
 cheese spread, cubed
Optional: grated Parmesan
 cheese

Cook pasta according to package directions; drain. Meanwhile, in a saucepan over medium heat, sauté green pepper, garlic and onion in olive oil until tender. Stir in tomato sauce, water and herbs. Reduce heat; simmer for 10 minutes. Transfer pasta to a large serving bowl; add cheese cubes and toss until melted. Pour tomato sauce mixture over pasta mixture; toss well. Serve immediately, sprinkled with Parmesan cheese, if desired. Serves 6.

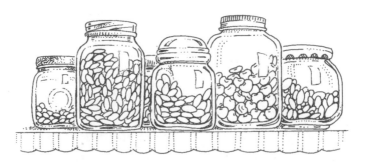

Watch for old-fashioned clear glass canisters at tag sales
and flea markets...perfect countertop storage for
macaroni, pasta and dried beans.

Simple Harvest
Supper

Mom's Mexican Mess

*Tamara Long
Huntsville, AR*

This recipe can be served in lots of different ways! Spoon it over tortilla chips for beefy nachos. Serve it in a bowl as a hearty dip. Use as burrito filling with flour tortillas. Or try it our favorite way, spooned over hot cornbread wedges and topped with black beans and sour cream, for a hot and hearty meal that's perfect after a cold football game night. Yummy!

1 lb. ground beef
1 onion, chopped
1 green pepper, chopped
2 cloves garlic, chopped
10-oz. can diced tomatoes with
   green chiles

1-1/4 oz. pkg. taco seasoning
   mix
8-oz. pkg. pasteurized process
   cheese spread, cubed
tortilla chips, flour tortillas or
   cornbread

Brown beef in a large skillet over medium heat; add onion, green pepper and garlic. Sauté until onion is translucent; drain. Add tomatoes with chiles, taco seasoning and cheese. Stir well; cook until cheese is melted. Serve as desired. Makes about 8 servings.

Feeding a crowd? Consider serving festive Mexican, Italian or Chinese-style dishes that everybody loves. They often feature rice or pasta, so they're filling yet easy on the pocketbook. The theme makes it a snap to put together the menu and table decorations too.

Creamy Chicken & Broccoli

Carol Van Rooy
Ontario, Canada

We love chicken and broccoli, so I especially like this satisfying
slow-cooker meal I can prep and walk away from.

10-3/4 oz. can cream of chicken
  soup
10-3/4 oz. can Cheddar cheese
  soup
14-oz. can chicken broth
1/4 t. Cajun seasoning

1/4 t. garlic salt
3 to 4 boneless, skinless chicken
  breasts
1 c. sour cream
6 c. broccoli flowerets, cooked
steamed rice

Combine soups, broth and seasonings in a slow cooker. Turn to low
setting; whisk until smooth. Add chicken to slow cooker, pushing
down into soup mixture. Cover and cook on low setting for 6 hours, or
on high setting for 3 hours. When chicken is very tender, use 2 forks
to shred into bite-size pieces. Return chicken to mixture in slow
cooker; stir in sour cream and cooked broccoli. To serve, spoon over
steamed rice. Serves 4 to 6.

Share the warmth. With winter on the way, autumn is a
perfect time to pull outgrown coats, hats and mittens
out of closets and donate them to a local charity.

Simple Harvest
Supper

Darlene's 5-Can Beef Stew

Darlene Marks
Youngstown, OH

I've shared this slow-cooker recipe with just about everyone I know! We all love it because it's comforting and delicious as well as easy to fix. Just add a fresh salad and some hearty bread.

1 lb. stew beef, cubed
14-1/2 oz. can diced tomatoes
14-1/2 oz. can green beans
15-1/4 oz. can corn
14-1/2 oz. can sliced carrots

14-1/2 oz. can diced new
   potatoes
1 c. brewed coffee
1-oz. pkg. onion soup mix

Place beef in a slow cooker. Pour all vegetables, without draining, over top. Add coffee to slow cooker; sprinkle soup mix over all. Mix gently with a large spoon. Cover and cook on low setting for 8 hours. Serves 4 to 6.

Stock up on favorite pantry items like vegetables, pasta and rice when they're on sale...they're oh-so handy for busy-day meals in a hurry.

Thyme Pork Chops

Denise Piccirilli
Huber Heights, OH

*Not only are these pork chops delicious, but they make
the whole house smell just wonderful!*

6 pork loin center-cut chops,
   1-inch thick
salt and pepper to taste

2 T. olive oil
1 T. fresh thyme, chopped, or
   1/2 t. dried thyme

Sprinkle pork chops on both sides with salt and plenty of pepper. In a
small bowl, stir together oil and thyme; brush over both sides of pork
chops. Arrange in a shallow roasting pan. Bake, uncovered, at
350 degrees for 50 to 60 minutes. Makes 6 servings.

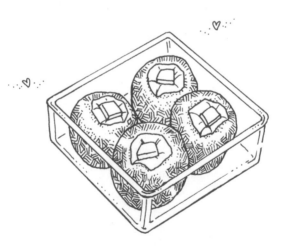

Baked apples are a scrumptious treat and go especially well
with pork. Core apples nearly through and place in a greased
baking pan. Fill each apple with a teaspoon of honey or maple
syrup, a teaspoon of butter and a little cinnamon. Bake at
350 degrees for 35 to 45 minutes, until tender. Serve warm,
topped with whipped cream...yummy!

Simple Harvest
Supper

Grandma's Special Pork Chops
Penny Derry
Boone, IA

Grandma & Grandpa always served this dish when we came to visit. Grandma often cooked on the oil burner in their dining room. The pork chops smelled so good! The sauce is wonderful spooned over mashed potatoes.

6 pork chops or loin cuts
Optional: 2 to 3 t. oil
4-oz. can sliced mushrooms,
   drained

1 onion, chopped
2 10-3/4 oz. cans cream of
   mushroom soup
salt and pepper to taste

Brown pork chops in a skillet over medium-high heat, using oil if skillet isn't non-stick. Arrange pork chops in a greased 13"x9" baking pan, overlapping as necessary. Spread mushrooms and onion over pork chops; spread soup over all. Sprinkle with salt and pepper. Cover and bake at 350 degrees for 45 minutes to one hour, checking occasionally for doneness. Serves 4 to 6.

Easy Cheesy Potatoes
Jane Gaither
North Lima, OH

When I made this for our annual Halloween party, the guys went wild over it! If you aren't serving a crowd, the recipe is simple to divide in half.

2 30-oz. pkgs. frozen shredded
   hashbrowns, thawed
16-oz. pkg. favorite-flavor
   shredded cheese

16-oz. container sour cream
1/2 c. butter, melted
1 to 2 c. milk

Place hashbrowns in a greased deep 13"x9" baking pan. Top with cheese; spread sour cream over cheese and drizzle with melted butter. Pour enough milk into pan to almost cover hashbrown mixture. Bake, uncovered, at 350 degrees for 45 minutes, or until a golden crust forms on top. Makes 8 to 10 servings.

Budget Turkey Sandwiches

Jody Strand
Baker, MT

This is my way to enjoy homemade turkey sandwiches when it isn't Thanksgiving. My son and his friends would rather have this sandwich than the whole big turkey dinner! If it is Thanksgiving, however, all you have to do is add shredded leftover turkey to the leftover dressing & gravy and press it in your loaf pan for tomorrow's fried turkey sandwiches. What could be easier?

2 turkey drumsticks
14-oz. can chicken broth
6-oz. pkg. turkey-flavored
   stuffing mix
Optional: 1/4 c. cornstarch,
   3/4 c. cold water

1 c. panko bread crumbs
2 to 3 t. oil
6 hoagie buns, split, toasted
   and buttered
Garnish: cranberry relish

Place drumsticks and broth in an oval slow cooker. Cover and cook on high setting for about 3 hours, until very tender. Remove drumsticks and let cool, reserving broth. Shred turkey with 2 forks and set aside, discarding skin and bones. Prepare stuffing mix according to package directions, using reserved broth instead of water. If mixture is too thin, shake cornstarch and water together in a jar; stir cornstarch mixture into stuffing. Add turkey to stuffing; mix together and press into a greased 9"x5" loaf pan. Cover and refrigerate overnight to set up. To serve, cut turkey loaf into thick slices; coat in bread crumbs. In a skillet over medium heat, fry slices in a little oil until crunchy, golden and heated through. Serve slices in buns, topped with cranberry relish. Serves 6.

October is crisp days and
cool nights, a time to curl up
around the dancing flames
and sink into a good book.

–John Sinor

Simple Harvest
Supper

Twice-Baked Sweet Potatoes

Tina Goodpasture
Meadowview, VA

My father and I love this side dish...it's like eating dessert!

2 sweet potatoes, halved
  lengthwise
1/4 c. Neufchâtel or cream
  cheese, cubed

2 T. milk
1 T. brown sugar, packed
1/4 t. cinnamon
1/4 c. chopped pecans

Place sweet potatoes cut-side down in an aluminum foil-lined 9"x9" baking pan. Bake, uncovered, at 425 degrees for 25 to 30 minutes, until tender and potatoes are pulling away from potato skins. Scoop potato pulp into a bowl, leaving 1/4-inch thick potato shells. Arrange potato shells in pan; set aside. Add cheese, milk, brown sugar and cinnamon to potato pulp; mash until blended. Spoon potato mixture into shells; top with nuts. Bake, uncovered, for 8 minutes, or until potatoes are heated through and nuts are toasted. Serves 4.

Old wooden bobbins make charming candleholders. Wind bobbins with yarn, choosing harvest shades of gold, orange and brown. Arrange bobbins in the center of your table, perch fat votives on top and surround with colorful gourds.

Corn & Spinach Casserole

Gloria Burd
Sunnyvale, CA

I got this recipe from my youngest sister, who doesn't really like to cook. This quick & easy casserole has been a smash hit at every potluck I have attended. Many times I've received a flurry of emails afterwards asking me for the recipe!

3-oz. can French fried onions, divided
8-oz. pkg. Monterey Jack or mozzarella cheese, sliced and divided

12-oz. pkg. frozen spinach soufflé, thawed
12-oz. pkg. frozen corn soufflé, thawed

Spray an 8"x8" baking pan with non-stick vegetable spray. Layer ingredients as follows: half of the onions, 1/3 of the cheese, all of the spinach soufflé, 1/3 of the cheese, all of the corn soufflé, remaining cheese and remaining onions. Bake, uncovered, at 350 degrees for 30 to 40 minutes, until golden. Makes 6 servings.

Before the first frost, save garden cuttings to brighten a sunny windowsill. Clip stems of impatiens or coleus, pull off most of the leaves and slip them into water-filled Mason jars. When roots form, plant the cuttings in potting soil and grow indoors until spring returns.

Simple Harvest
Supper

Gingery Glazed Carrots

Marcia Marcoux
Charlton, MA

*A no-fuss way to dress up baby carrots. Try it with honey
instead of brown sugar too.*

1/4 c. brown sugar, packed	1/2 t. ground ginger
1/2 c. butter, sliced	1/4 t. cinnamon
1 t. salt	16-oz. pkg. baby carrots

In a large saucepan over medium heat, combine all ingredients. Cover
and simmer, stirring occasionally, until carrots are tender, 20 to
30 minutes. Serves 6 to 8.

For a quick & easy table runner, choose seasonal cotton fabric
printed with autumn leaves and Indian corn in glowing gold,
orange and brown. Simply pink the edges...it will dress up
the dinner table all season long!

Hearty Beef Macaroni

Libby Case
Louisville, KY

My grandmother made this dish for dinner whenever all the grandchildren came over for a visit. It's terrific for game-day parties too.

32-oz. pkg. elbow macaroni,
  uncooked
1-1/2 lbs. ground beef round
1 onion, chopped

15-oz. can tomato sauce
15-oz. can diced tomatoes with
  green chiles
salt and pepper to taste

Cook macaroni according to package directions; drain and return to cooking pot. Meanwhile, in a large skillet over medium heat, cook beef and onion until browned; drain. Add beef mixture and remaining ingredients to macaroni. Cook over low heat for 15 minutes, until heated through. May also be made in a slow cooker. Combine cooked macaroni, beef mixture and remaining ingredients in a slow cooker. Cover and cook on low setting for 2 hours. Makes 10 servings.

Give favorite pasta recipes a twist for fall...pick up some pasta in seasonal shapes like autumn leaves, pumpkins or turkeys! Some even come in veggie colors like orange, red or green.

Simple Harvest
Supper

Cheesy Chili Dog Bake

Kristy Scruggs
Ringgold, GA

Easy and yummy! Our family's favorite meal whenever we're watching the big game together.

9 hot dog buns, cut up
9 hot dogs, cut up
2 16-oz. cans chili with beans

1/2 c. onion, chopped
1/2 c. green onions, chopped
2 c. shredded Cheddar cheese

In a lightly greased 13"x9" baking pan, layer bun pieces, then hot dog pieces. Pour chili over hot dogs; sprinkle with onion, green onions and cheese. Bake, uncovered, at 350 degrees for 30 minutes, or until hot and bubbly. Makes 8 servings.

If you often use chopped onion, celery and green pepper to add flavor to sautéed dishes, save time by chopping lots at once. Create your own sauté blend and freeze it in a plastic freezer container. Add it to skillet dishes straight from the freezer...there's no need to thaw.

Easy Stuffed Manicotti

Barbara Brazelton
Arlington, NE

My go-to recipe when I get home from work! It's so easy to make...
and everyone thinks you spent a lot of time stuffing the manicotti.

8-oz. pkg. manicotti pasta
    shells, uncooked
1 lb. ground beef
1/2 c. onion, chopped
28-oz. jar spaghetti sauce,
    divided

14 pieces string cheese
1-1/2 c. shredded mozzarella
    cheese

Cook manicotti according to package directions; drain. Meanwhile, in
a large skillet over medium heat, cook beef and onion until beef is no
longer pink; drain. Stir in spaghetti sauce. Spread half of beef mixture
in a greased 13"x9" baking pan. Stuff each manicotti shell with a piece
of string cheese. Arrange shells in pan; top with remaining beef
mixture. Cover and bake at 350 degrees for 25 to 30 minutes, or until
heated through. Sprinkle with mozzarella cheese. Bake, uncovered, for
5 to 10 minutes, until cheese is melted. Makes 4 to 5 servings.

If you're traveling "over the river and through the woods"
for Thanksgiving, make a trip bag for each of the kids...a special
tote bag that's filled with favorite small toys, puzzles and other
fun stuff, reserved just for road trips. The miles are sure
to speed by much faster!

Simple Harvest
Supper

Lazy Lasagna

Donna Henricks
Mesa, AZ

When we lived in Ohio, we had neighborhood parties often. This was one of our favorites from those days...it still is. Can't stay out of it...even a spoonful cold from the fridge is yummy!

8-oz. pkg. medium egg noodles,
   uncooked
1-1/2 lbs. ground beef
seasoning salt to taste
8-oz. pkg. cream cheese, cubed

1 c. cottage cheese
1 c. sour cream
15-oz. can tomato sauce
Garnish: grated Parmesan
   cheese

Cook noodles according to package directions; drain. Meanwhile, in a large skillet over medium heat, brown beef. Drain; sprinkle to taste with seasoning salt. Combine beef and noodles with remaining ingredients except Parmesan cheese. Transfer to a lightly greased deep 13"x9" baking pan; sprinkle with Parmesan cheese. Bake, uncovered, at 375 degrees for 45 minutes. Let stand for a few minutes before serving. Makes 8 to 10 servings.

Let the kids invite a special friend or two home for dinner.
Keep it simple with a hearty casserole like Lazy Lasagna and
a relish tray of crunchy veggies & dip. A great way to
get to know your children's playmates!

Gobble-Good Turkey Bake

Michelle Zubalik
Kingsley, MI

The last day of school before Thanksgiving, my son's second-grade teacher Mrs. Way sent home a baggie of rice with this recipe attached. It's a perfect dish for leftover turkey...and so easy to prepare, my seven-year-old made it himself. Everyone in the family loved it, even the picky eaters. Thank you, Mrs. Way!

10-3/4 oz. can cream of
    mushroom soup
10-3/4 oz. can cream of celery
    soup

1-1/2 c. milk
1-oz. pkg. onion soup mix
1 c. long-cooking rice, uncooked
2 to 3 c. cooked turkey, cubed

Combine all ingredients in a lightly greased 13"x9" baking pan; stir. Cover and bake at 350 degrees for 45 minutes, or until hot and rice is tender. Serves 6.

When making a favorite casserole, it's easy to make a double batch. After baking, let the extra casserole cool, then wrap it and tuck it in the freezer...ready to share with a new mother, carry to a potluck or reheat on a busy night at home.

Simple Harvest
Supper

Cranberry-Pear Tossed Salad

Ronna Farley
Rockville, MD

My husband and I love this fruity salad! It was inspired by a salad we ate at our son's wedding several years ago. It is perfect for autumn...delicious and so easy to prepare.

4 c. arugula lettuce mix
1 pear, cored and sliced
1/2 c. sweetened dried
   cranberries

1/2 c. pumpkin seeds
1/2 c. raspberry-walnut salad
   dressing, or to taste

Divide lettuce mix among 4 salad plates. Top with pear slices, cranberries and pumpkin seeds. Drizzle with salad dressing. Serve immediately. Makes 4 servings.

There are lots of tasty choices for crisp autumn salads. Start with cool-weather greens like romaine lettuce, endive, fennel, Swiss chard and cabbage. Add crunchy apple slices or tender diced pears, a sprinkling of nuts or seeds and perhaps some crumbled feta or blue cheese. Drizzle with a fruity vinaigrette...delicious!

Favorite Apricot Chicken

Carol Beecher
Adelanto, CA

This is a recipe I found in a magazine years ago and it's requested often by my family. Orange marmalade or raspberry preserves and Russian salad dressing can be substituted...it always turns out yummy and it is sooo easy to make!

6 chicken breasts, or your
    favorite pieces
1 c. apricot preserves

1-oz. pkg. onion soup mix
1 c. Italian salad dressing

Remove skin from chicken, if desired. Arrange chicken in a greased 13"x9" baking pan. Dollop preserves over chicken; sprinkle with soup mix and drizzle with salad dressing. Cover with aluminum foil. Bake at 350 degrees for 45 minutes to one hour, until chicken juices run clear when pierced. Makes 6 servings.

When I was a child, my grandfather operated an apple orchard in western North Carolina. My mom tells me that one day I went missing. They finally found me in the barn where the picked apples were stored. I'd found a crate of apples and taken a bite out of nearly every apple. Someone asked me what I was doing and I told them I was "looking for the best 'papple' Papaw had." Nowadays when I start seeing apples from North Carolina at my local supermarket, I stop, take in the scent...and I am instantly carried back to my grandfather's apple orchard.

–Sophia Graves, Okeechobee, FL

Simple Harvest
Supper

Apple & Orange Slaw

Charlene Letterly
Leesburg, FL

This salad recipe is terrific for guests and potlucks...it is quick & easy and lots of people like it!

1-1/2 c. cabbage, shredded
10-oz. can mandarin oranges, drained
1 Red Delicious apple, cored and diced

1/2 c. fat-free mayonnaise
1 T. brown sugar, packed

Place cabbage, oranges and apple in a serving bowl; toss to combine. In a small bowl, mix together mayonnaise and brown sugar; add to cabbage mixture and stir to coat well. Cover and chill one hour before serving. Makes 4 servings.

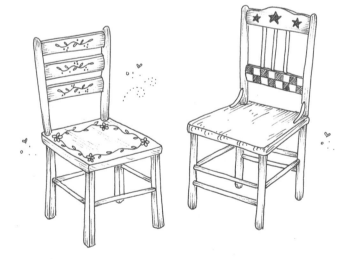

Savor warm, sunny Indian summer days on the porch. Spruce up your outdoor chairs or pull together mismatched yard-sale finds...it's simple! Spray-paint them all the same color or use a rainbow of colors just for fun.

Savory Pork Roast

Cherilyn Dunn
Fairborn, OH

We live in the country, and this hearty slow-cooker recipe hits the spot after a day of working on the farm. To make this a one-pot meal, I put five peeled and cubed potatoes and a cup of baby carrots into the slow cooker before adding the roast.

4 to 5-lb. pork roast
1/2 t. salt
1/4 t. pepper
1 clove garlic, slivered
2 onions, sliced and divided

2 bay leaves
1 whole clove
1/2 c. hot water
1 T. soy sauce

Rub roast with salt and pepper. Make tiny slits in surface of roast with a sharp knife tip; insert garlic slivers. Place roast in a broiler pan. Broil 15 to 20 minutes, until roast is browned and excess fat is removed. Add one sliced onion to the bottom of a large slow cooker. Top with roast, remaining onion and other ingredients. Cover and cook on low setting for 10 hours, or high for 5 to 6 hours. Discard bay leaves and clove before serving. Serves 6.

Let everyone know what's inside each dish at the next buffet or potluck. Write each dish's name on a beautiful real or faux autumn leaf using a gold or silver metallic marker.

Simple Harvest Supper

Ginger Ale Baked Apples

Judy Lange
Imperial, PA

A yummy fall dessert or after-the-game snack!

4 baking apples
1/4 c. golden raisins, divided
4 t. brown sugar, packed and
   divided

1/2 c. ginger ale

Core apples but do not cut through the bottoms. Place apples in an ungreased 8"x8" baking pan. Spoon one tablespoon raisins and one teaspoon brown sugar into the center of each apple. Pour ginger ale over apples. Bake, uncovered, at 350 degrees, basting occasionally, for 45 minutes, or until apples are tender. Serve warm or cold. Serves 4.

Make the sweetest harvest of "acorns" in a jiffy! With a dab of frosting, attach a mini vanilla wafer to a milk chocolate drop. Add a "stem" made from a bit of pretzel. Fill a bowl for nibbling, or top each dinner plate with three or four acorns.

Feta Cheese Tossed Salad

Holly Child
Parker, CO

This simple salad is packed with a lot of flavor
thanks to the feta cheese and walnuts.

1 head green leaf lettuce, torn
    into bite-size pieces
8-oz. container crumbled feta
    cheese
3/4 c. chopped walnuts

3 to 4 stalks celery, finely
    chopped
1/2 t. pepper
2 T. oil
2 T. white vinegar

In a salad bowl, combine all ingredients except oil and vinegar. Toss to mix. Drizzle oil and vinegar over salad; toss again. Cover and refrigerate for at least one hour. Serve chilled. Makes 4 to 6 servings.

For an autumn centerpiece that only takes a moment, place a white Lumina pumpkin on a cake stand and tuck some bittersweet sprigs around it. Simple yet so eye-catching.

Simple Harvest
Supper

Cranberry Frappe

Laura Hall
Rolla, MO

Every year for Thanksgiving and Christmas, my Nana would make Cranberry Frappe. I remember standing in the kitchen with her as a little girl and waiting for those cranberries to "pop!" Since she's gone, I stand at the stove and imagine my Nana standing next to me. This dish is delicious as either a side or a dessert and a handy make-ahead.

2 c. fresh cranberries	1 t. unflavored gelatin
4-1/2 c. water, divided	juice of 1 lemon
1-1/2 c. sugar	

Place cranberries and 4 cups water in a saucepan. Boil over medium heat for 10 to 15 minutes, until cranberries have popped; do not drain. Pour cranberry mixture through a sieve into a bowl, reserving juice; discard berry pulp. While juice is still hot, add sugar; stir until sugar dissolves. In a cup, soften gelatin in remaining water; add to cranberry juice along with lemon juice. Pour mixture into a metal bowl; cover and freeze 8 hours to overnight. With an electric mixer on medium speed, beat until fluffy. Return to freezer until mixture is almost a sorbet consistency. Serves 8 to 10.

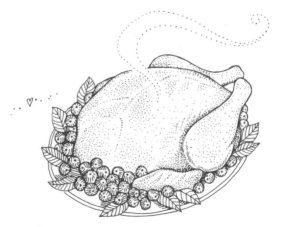

Enjoy tried & true recipes at Thanksgiving this year,
but toss in a new one just for fun...you never know,
it just might turn out to be a family favorite!

Lemon-Chive Butter

Andrea Heyart
Aubrey, TX

I love to use this scrumptious butter to roast chicken and turkey, to flavor pastas, baked potatoes, steamed rice and fresh veggies or just to spread on a warm dinner roll!

1 c. butter, softened   juice of 2 lemons
1/4 c. fresh chives, minced

In a bowl, combine all ingredients and stir until well blended. Cover tightly. May also be formed into a log. Using a spatula, place butter mixture on a sheet of wax paper and roll up tightly, jelly-roll fashion. Chill for one hour before serving; may be kept refrigerated up to one week. Makes one cup.

Small-town harvest festivals are full of old-fashioned fun...where else could you eat a pumpkin burger or cheer on an antique tractor pull? Check with your state's tourism office for a list of seasonal festivals and fairs in your area, then pick one and go!

Thanksgiving
with All the
Trimmings

Holiday Brined Turkey

Sharon Demers
Dolores, CO

My husband and I first tried brined turkey several years ago and fell in love with it. Since then, we've experimented to come up with this flavorful mix of herbs and spices. We hope you'll enjoy it too!

1 gal. boiling water
18 to 20-lb. turkey, thawed

1 gal. cold water

Add Turkey Brine Mix to boiling water. Cool thoroughly; chill. Place turkey and brining liquid in a very large container. Add enough cold water to cover turkey. Keep refrigerated or on ice for 12 to 24 hours. Before roasting turkey, rinse well with cold water and pat dry. Roast as desired. Makes enough brine mix for an 18 to 20-pound turkey.

Turkey Brine Mix:

1 c. coarse sea salt
1/2 c. brown sugar, packed
1 T. sweetened dried
   cranberries, finely chopped
1 T. orange zest
1 T. dried apples, chopped

2 t. peppercorns
1/2 t. dried thyme
1/2 t. dried sage
1/2 t. dried rosemary
1/8 t. garlic powder
3 shakes red pepper flakes

Combine all ingredients; mix well. Use immediately or store in a covered container.

Gourds and mini pumpkins left over from Halloween can do double duty on the Thanksgiving table. Spray them gold with craft paint and tuck into harvest centerpieces.

Granny's Cornbread Dressing

Susan Butterworth
Harper, TX

For years I watched my mother as she made this dressing. I was the official "dressing tester"...the more sage, the better! I was a baby when Grandmother died and Mom has been gone a couple of years now, but every Thanksgiving & Christmas when I make the dressing, I feel as though Mom's right there with me.

6-1/4 c. cornbread, crumbled
2-1/2 c. chicken broth
1/2 c. butter, melted
1/2 c. onion, chopped
1-1/4 c. celery, chopped

3 T. oil
1 t. seasoned salt
1 t. pepper
5 t. dried sage, or more to taste
3 to 4 eggs, well beaten

In a large bowl, combine cornbread, broth and butter. Mix well and set aside. In a skillet over medium heat, sauté onion and celery in oil until softened, 4 to 5 minutes. Add onion mixture to cornbread mixture along with seasonings; mix well. Let stand for 15 minutes. Fold eggs into cornbread mixture; transfer to a greased 2-quart casserole dish. Bake, uncovered, at 375 degrees for 50 to 65 minutes, until top is golden. Serves 12 to 14.

Homemade gravy is a must at Thanksgiving and it's simple to make. Remove the roast turkey to a platter. Set the roasting pan with pan juices on a stove burner over medium heat. In a small jar, shake together 1/4 cup cold water and 1/4 cup cornstarch; pour into the pan. Cook and stir until gravy boils and thickens, 5 to 10 minutes. Add salt and pepper to taste and it's ready to serve.

Brown Sugar Glazed Ham
Vickie

I like to offer a choice of roast turkey and baked ham when my family gathers for Thanksgiving. They all like this ham! There's plenty left for yummy sandwiches the next day too.

8-lb. fully-cooked boneless ham
1/2 c. brown sugar, packed
2 T. cornstarch
1 c. water
Optional: 1/4 c. brandy

3 T. lemon juice
1 t. Dijon mustard
1 t. ground ginger
1/4 t. cinnamon
1/2 c. golden raisins

Place ham in a large roasting pan. Bake, uncovered, at 325 degrees for one hour. Meanwhile, in a saucepan over medium heat, combine brown sugar, cornstarch, water and brandy, if using. Cook, stirring constantly, until glaze is clear and thickened. Stir in remaining ingredients. Remove ham from oven; discard drippings in pan. Spoon glaze over ham; return to oven. Bake an additional 30 minutes, basting occasionally with glaze from pan. Let stand a few minutes before slicing. Makes 12 to 15 servings.

Thanksgiving Day is a terrific time to catch up on the past year with family & friends. Set up a family memory table and ask everybody to bring along snapshots, clippings, even Junior's soccer trophy and Betty Lou's latest knitting project... you'll all have so much to talk about!

Sweet Potatoes in Baskets

Tricia Thompson
Moorefield, WV

My mother made this recipe every year for Thanksgiving dinner. I have such fond memories of cooking with her. These sweet potatoes are good with both turkey and ham, and they look so pretty on the dining table.

3 c. sweet potatoes, peeled, cooked and mashed
1/2 t. salt
1/2 t. lemon zest
1/2 t. cinnamon
1/4 t. ground cloves
1/4 t. ground ginger

1/4 to 1/2 c. brown sugar, packed
2 eggs, beaten
6 navel oranges
Garnish: marshmallows, or walnut or pecan halves

In a bowl, combine sweet potatoes, seasonings, brown sugar and eggs. Mix thoroughly; set aside. Cut tops off oranges in zig-zag style, leaving shells intact. Scoop out orange pulp with a spoon. Fill scooped-out orange shells with sweet potato mixture, adding some of the orange pulp if mixture is too thick. Place oranges in an ungreased baking pan. Bake, uncovered, at 350 degrees for 25 to 30 minutes. Top each with a marshmallow or a nut half; return to oven for 2 minutes, until golden. Makes 6 servings.

If time is tight, streamline your holiday plans...just ask your family what festive foods and traditions they cherish the most. Then focus on tried & true activities and free up time to try something new.

Harvest-Time Pork Loin

Sunni Starkes
Athens, TX

When I traveled to China to bring back my adopted daughter, I made friends with three other women in my group. The first autumn home with our daughters, they all came to Vermont to spend a weekend with us. We spent the day savoring the crisp fall air and watching our beautiful daughters picking up the bright fall leaves. We came back to our log cabin filled with the delicious smell of this meal cooking.

1-lb. boneless pork tenderloin
4 c. apple cider
1 t. cinnamon
1 t. nutmeg
7-oz. pkg. dried apricots
3 apples, peeled, cored and cut
into wedges

Place pork loin in a Dutch oven over low heat. Add cider and spices; stir. Cover and simmer at least one hour. Add apricots, making sure they are covered with cider; cover and continue cooking for one hour. Shortly before serving, add apples; cover and cook about 15 minutes, until apples are soft. Remove pork and apples to a serving platter; keep warm. Cook cider mixture in Dutch oven over high heat, stirring occasionally, for about 10 minutes, until reduced to a medium glaze consistency. Slice pork and arrange on a platter surrounded by apples. Spoon glaze over apples; serve immediately. Serves 4.

Slow-Cooker Method:

Combine pork loin, cider and spices in a slow cooker. Cover and cook on low setting for 7 hours; add apricots and continue cooking for one hour. Shortly before serving, transfer contents of slow cooker to a Dutch oven. Add apples; cover and cook over medium heat for 15 minutes, until soft. Remove pork and apples to a platter; finish as directed above.

Come, ye thankful people, come,
Raise the song of harvest home!

–Henry Alford

Thanksgiving with All the Trimmings

Asparagus Bundles

Mary Ann Dimick
Bowling Green, OH

Not everyone in our family likes asparagus, so I looked for ways to enhance the flavor of our garden-fresh spears. Now these bundles are requested for the holidays and even as party appetizers.

1 bunch thin asparagus spears,
    trimmed to 6-inch lengths
1 to 2 T. olive oil

kosher salt and cracked pepper
    to taste
6 to 8 slices bacon, halved

In a large bowl, combine asparagus, olive oil, salt and pepper. Mix gently with your hands; let stand several minutes. For each bundle, wrap 3 to 4 spears with a piece of bacon; lay on an ungreased rimmed baking sheet. Bake, uncovered, at 400 degrees for 12 to 15 minutes, until asparagus is tender and bacon is crisp. Serve warm or at room temperature. Makes 4 to 6 servings.

Roasted Brussels Sprouts

Stacy Kaegi
Wappingers Falls, NY

A must-have for holiday meals...yum!

2 lbs. Brussels sprouts, trimmed
    and halved
1 c. pecans, coarsely chopped
2 T. olive oil

2 cloves garlic, finely chopped
1/2 t. kosher salt
1/4 t. pepper

Toss together all ingredients on a large rimmed baking sheet. Turn Brussels sprouts cut-side down. Bake, uncovered, at 400 degrees for 20 to 25 minutes, until golden and tender. Serves 6.

Younger guests will feel oh-so grown up when served bubbly sparkling cider in long-stemmed plastic glasses. Decorate with curling ribbon just for fun.

No-Noodle Eggplant Lasagna
Angie Womack
Cave City, AR

My husband and youngest son are diabetic, so I'm always on the lookout for festive low-carb main dishes. This one has been quite a success! It freezes very well, so I can portion it into freezer containers for my son to take back to college.

1 large eggplant, peeled and
    sliced 1/4-inch thick
1 T. olive oil
1 lb. ground beef
4-oz. can sliced mushrooms,
    drained
8-oz. can tomato sauce
6-oz. can tomato paste
1/2 c. water

1 t. dried oregano
1 t. garlic powder
salt and pepper to taste
8-oz. container ricotta cheese
1 c. grated Parmesan cheese
3 eggs, beaten
Garnish: additional grated
    Parmesan cheese

Place eggplant slices in a single layer on a greased baking sheet. Brush tops with olive oil. Bake at 400 degrees for 15 minutes, or until tender; cool. Meanwhile, in a large skillet over medium heat, brown beef and drain. Stir in mushrooms, tomato sauce, tomato paste, water and seasonings. Simmer over medium heat until thickened. In a bowl, combine remaining ingredients except garnish; mix well. Coat a 13"x9" baking pan with non-stick vegetable spray. Layer half each of beef mixture, cheese mixture and eggplant slices. Repeat layers; top with more Parmesan cheese. Bake, uncovered, at 350 degrees for 40 minutes, or until heated through and golden on top. Serves 6.

Be sure to have some take-out containers and labels on hand to send everyone home with leftovers...if there are any!

Saucy Barbecue Hens

Diane Widmer
Blue Island, IL

Thirty years ago when I'd just started to cook "real" food, I came up with this recipe for Easter. My family loved barbecue and I wanted to make something besides ham. This was a hit!

4 Cornish hens, thawed   salt and pepper to taste

Sprinkle hens inside and out with salt and pepper. Arrange in a shallow baking pan. Bake, uncovered, at 350 degrees for about one hour, until crisp and juices run clear when pierced, basting frequently with Barbecue Sauce. If hens are over 18 ounces, bake for one hour and 15 minutes, basting after 15 minutes. Serves 4 to 8.

Barbecue Sauce:

1 c. catsup   2 T. steak sauce
6-oz. can tomato paste   1 T. mustard
1/2 c. brown sugar, packed   1 t. Worcestershire sauce
1/3 c. cider vinegar   1/4 t. garlic powder

Combine all ingredients in a saucepan over medium heat. Bring to a boil; simmer 5 to 8 minutes, stirring often.

Make the children's table special! On a cotton tablecloth, let the kids trace around their hands with paint pens or permanent markers, then turn the handprints into turkeys. Be sure to have them sign and date their turkeys. A sweet tradition that can be added to each year.

Maple Baked Beans

Taylor Morris
Oregon City, OR

This recipe was first given to me by my grandma to make for Thanksgiving. I like to change it up a bit each year, and it's always a favorite. Sometimes I'll opt for honey rather than maple syrup.

1 lb. ground beef
2 16-oz. cans maple baked
   beans
15-oz. can pork & beans
1 green pepper, diced

1 to 2 T. picante hot sauce
1 t. maple syrup
1 t. ground cumin
1/2 t. dry mustard
salt and pepper to taste

Brown beef in a Dutch oven over medium heat; drain. Add remaining ingredients; stir together. Cover and bake at 400 degrees for one to 1-1/2 hours, stirring occasionally, until beans are thickened and bubbly. Makes 8 to 10 servings.

I grew up in a Norwegian household and Scandinavian traditions were held sacred. Every Thanksgiving our family would bundle up and drive 50 miles to visit our relatives in Watertown, South Dakota. Sometimes, because of unpredictable weather, we would have to stay overnight. It was quite an adventure for me as we would play cards and games late into the night and I got to stay up past my bedtime. I remember during the most terrible blizzards we still slept with the window cracked open...my relatives loved fresh air! The room was freezing, but we were so cozy, cuddled under warm feather quilts. The morning after Thanksgiving, our hosts would wake us with traditional egg coffee and a plate of yummy marshmallow bars. I have so many happy memories of those times!

–Paula Coome, Sioux Falls, SD

Brown Sugar-Bacon Squash

Cindy Jamieson
Ontario, Canada

I fell in love with this recipe while working at a restaurant with my friend. A few months later, we started dating and have been together for ten years. It's one of the few ways I like to eat squash. By the way, here in Ontario we call them pepper squash!

1 acorn squash, peeled, halved
   and seeds removed
1/3 c. butter

salt and pepper to taste
1 c. brown sugar, packed
8 slices bacon, halved

Cut each squash half into quarters and cut each quarter in half, to create 16 pieces. Place squash skin-side down on an aluminum foil-lined rimmed baking sheet. Top each piece with one teaspoon butter, salt, pepper, one tablespoon brown sugar and 1/2 slice bacon. Bake, uncovered, at 350 degrees for 30 to 45 minutes, until bacon is crisp and squash is tender. Serves 8.

Wrap glass votives with cinnamon sticks or autumn leaves, secured with a rubber band. Hide the rubber band with strands of raffia and tuck in votive candles. Set one at each guest's place or march them down the center of the table...so pretty!

Carrots & Cheese Casserole

Carole Rhoades
Galena, OH

Just the thought of this delicious recipe warms my heart! It came from my cousin's wife Barb 20 years ago. If time is short, you can use canned sliced carrots...they won't need to be cooked.

4 c. carrots, peeled and sliced
1 onion, minced
3/4 to 1-1/4 c. butter, divided
1/4 c. all-purpose flour
1 t. salt
1/4 t. dry mustard

2 c. milk
1/4 t. celery salt
1/8 t. pepper
8-oz. pkg. shredded sharp
   Cheddar cheese
3 c. soft bread crumbs

In a saucepan over medium heat, cover carrots with salted water. Cook until barely tender, 10 to 15 minutes; drain and set aside. In a separate skillet over medium heat, cook onion in 1/4 cup butter for 2 to 3 minutes. Stir in flour, salt and mustard. Add milk; cook, stirring constantly, until smooth. Stir in celery salt and pepper. In a greased 2-quart casserole dish, arrange 2 to 3 layers of carrots and cheese, ending with carrots. Pour onion mixture over carrots. Melt desired amount of remaining butter and toss with bread crumbs; sprinkle crumbs over top. Bake, uncovered, at 350 degrees for 35 minutes. Serves 8.

There's always room for one more at the harvest table. Why not invite a neighbor or a college student who might be spending the holiday alone to share your Thanksgiving feast?

Scalloped Celery

Kellie Ford
Ashland, NE

This yummy recipe was given to me by my sister-in-law Sara. She used to make it for Thanksgiving dinner when the whole family got together. It's still a favorite of mine.

2 c. celery, chopped
8-oz. can sliced water chestnuts, drained
4 c. water
1/2 c. onion, chopped
1/3 c. butter, divided

10-3/4 oz. can cream of chicken soup
20 round buttery crackers, coarsely crushed
Garnish: slivered almonds

In a saucepan over medium heat, cook celery and water chestnuts in water about 10 minutes. Drain and set aside. In a skillet over medium heat, sauté onion in one tablespoon butter until tender. Combine celery mixture, onion mixture and soup; transfer to a greased 1-1/2 quart casserole dish. Sprinkle cracker crumbs over top; dot with remaining butter. Bake, uncovered, at 350 degrees for 20 minutes. Sprinkle with almonds and bake 15 minutes longer. Makes 8 servings.

Lay a colorful paper leaf cut-out on each dinner plate. Invite guests to write something on their leaf that they're thankful for. Afterwards, attach all the leaves to a wreath form with hot glue. Sure to be cherished!

Bratwurst Meatloaf

Trysha Mapley
Palmer, AK

My family agrees this meatloaf is simply awesome. Wonderful German flavor perfect with mashed potatoes for a truly homey meal. We never have leftovers on this one!

1 lb. lean ground beef
1 lb. bratwurst, removed from
   casings and broken up
1 c. soft bread crumbs
2 cloves garlic, pressed
1-oz. pkg. onion soup mix
8-oz. can tomato sauce
1 egg, beaten

2 T. flat-leaf parsley, chopped
2 T. mustard
1 T. cider vinegar
celery salt and pepper to taste
Garnish: additional mustard
5 slices bacon
1 T. brown sugar, packed

In a large bowl, mix together all ingredients except garnish, bacon and brown sugar. Press into a 9"x5" loaf pan sprayed with non-stick vegetable spray. Spread additional mustard over meatloaf. Arrange bacon slices over top; trim bacon or tuck in the edges on the sides. Press brown sugar onto bacon. Cover and bake at 350 degrees for one hour. Drain off any excess fat; let meatloaf rest 5 minutes before slicing. Serves 8.

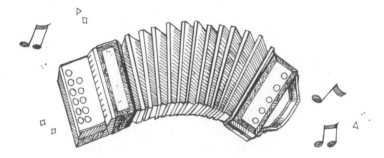

Throw an Oktoberfest party for family & friends. Set a festive mood with polka music. Toss some brats on the grill to serve in hard rolls...don't forget the spicy mustard! Round out the menu with potato salad, homemade applesauce and German chocolate cake for dessert.

Thanksgiving with All the Trimmings

Braised Cabbage & Apples

Gail Blain Prather
Hastings, NE

A scrumptious fall side dish that goes well with roast pork, pork chops or grilled sausages. Use red or green cabbage, or a mixture of both.

3 slices bacon
1 yellow onion, peeled and
    thinly sliced
1 head cabbage, shredded
1/2 c. cider vinegar
1/2 c. apple cider

1/2 c. sugar
4 whole cloves
2 tart apples, peeled, cored and
    thinly sliced
salt and pepper to taste

Cook bacon in a large, deep skillet over medium heat until crisp. Drain bacon on paper towels, reserving drippings in skillet. Crumble bacon and set aside. Sauté onion in reserved drippings over medium heat until tender and golden. In a bowl, toss cabbage with vinegar; add to skillet along with remaining ingredients except salt and pepper. Simmer, uncovered, over low heat until cabbage is tender, about 20 minutes. Discard cloves. Season to taste with salt and pepper; serve garnished with crumbled bacon. Serves 6.

A hot cup of flavored coffee is oh-so welcome after a hearty meal. Simply add a few drops of almond or cinnamon extract to the ground coffee in the percolator basket before brewing.

Delicious Bacon Turkey

Kim Jewett
Highland, UT

The first year I tried this, my son-in-law declared it's the only way
I should roast our turkey from now on! It makes a moist
and smoky flavored turkey, and it's so simple to do.

12 to 14-lb. turkey, thawed   16-oz. pkg. bacon

Place turkey in a roasting pan. Cover breast portion with slices of
bacon; tent with aluminum foil. Bake at 350 degrees for about 3 to
3-1/2 hours, until a meat thermometer reads 165 degrees. One hour
before turkey is done, remove foil and remove bacon to allow turkey
to become golden. Serves 10 to 12.

Herbed Potato Gratin

Joan White
Malvern, PA

If you're looking for an easy, elegant, delicious potato dish for a
holiday meal, try this one. The flavored cheese perfectly seasons
the potatoes with just enough garlic.

2 to 4 T. butter, melted   2 c. whipping cream
3 lbs. redskin potatoes, peeled   5-oz. container soft cheese
   and thinly sliced   with garlic & herbs
salt and pepper to taste

Spread butter in a 13"x9" baking pan. Arrange half of sliced potatoes
in pan; season generously with salt and pepper. In a large heavy
saucepan over medium heat, stir cream and cheese until mixture is
smooth. Pour half of cheese mixture over potatoes in pan. Arrange
remaining potatoes on top; season with more salt and pepper. Pour
remaining cream mixture over potatoes. Bake, uncovered, at
400 degrees for about one hour, until golden and potatoes are
tender. Serves 8.

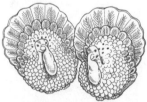

Vintage turkey salt & pepper shakers
brighten any autumn tabletop.

Thanksgiving with All the Trimmings

Icebox Mashed Potatoes

Pat Martin
Riverside, CA

These potatoes are delicious with gravy, but really don't need any topping because they are so creamy and good! I've used this recipe for Thanksgiving for over 30 years. It's a wonderful make-ahead dish and travels well too.

5 lbs. baking potatoes, peeled and halved
2 t. chicken bouillon granules
1/2 t. garlic salt
16-oz. container low-fat sour cream

8-oz. pkg. reduced-fat cream cheese
2 t. onion powder
2 t. salt
1/4 t. pepper
2 T. butter, sliced

Cover potatoes with water in a deep stockpot; add bouillon and garlic salt. Bring to a boil over high heat; cook until potatoes are tender, about 20 minutes. Remove from heat; drain into a colander. Return potatoes to the same pot and mash. Add remaining ingredients except butter; mix well. Spoon potatoes into a greased 13"x9" baking pan; dot with butter. Cool slightly; cover with plastic wrap and refrigerate up to 3 days. To serve, let stand at room temperature for 30 minutes. Uncover; bake at 350 degrees for 40 minutes. If top browns too quickly, cover with aluminum foil for the last 10 minutes. May also be reheated in a microwave oven on 80% power for 30 minutes, rotating occasionally. Makes 10 to 12 servings.

One of the best ways to give thanks is to help someone else. Volunteer, lend a neighbor a hand, leave a surprise on someone's doorstep...there are lots of thoughtful ways to show you care.

Broccoli-Corn Casserole

Denise Hennebury
Greensboro, NC

In 1976, my husband and I were alone for Thanksgiving in Vermont. We lived in the lower level of an old farmhouse, and our upstairs neighbors, another young couple who were alone for the holiday, invited us for dinner. Our hostess served this wonderful side dish, and she was kind enough to share the recipe with me. I have made this delicious casserole dozens of times since then...I have yet to find someone who doesn't love it!

10-oz. pkg. frozen chopped broccoli	1/4 t. salt
	1/8 t. pepper
16-oz. can cream-style corn	3 T. butter
1 egg, lightly beaten	1-2/3 c. herb-seasoned stuffing
1 T. onion, minced	mix, divided

Cook or microwave broccoli for about one minute; break apart. In a bowl, mix broccoli and remaining ingredients except butter and stuffing mix; set aside. Melt butter in a saucepan over low heat. Add stuffing mix; toss to mix and remove from heat immediately. Stir one cup stuffing mixture into broccoli mixture. Turn into an ungreased 1-1/2 quart casserole dish; sprinkle with remaining stuffing mixture. Bake, uncovered, at 350 degrees for 35 to 40 minutes, until top is golden. Serves 4 to 6.

A day or two before Thanksgiving, set out all the serving platters, baskets and dishes and label them..."Roast Turkey," "Grandma's Dinner Rolls" and so on. When the big day arrives, you'll be able to put dinner on the table in no time at all.

Corn, Lima & Tomato Bake

Michelle Marberry
Valley, AL

This hot, hearty veggie dish is a scrumptious change from plain old succotash. Try it in the summertime too... it's even better made with fresh veggies!

8 slices bacon, divided
16-oz. pkg. frozen lima beans
1 lb. tomatoes, sliced and
   divided

1 onion, chopped
1 green pepper, chopped
16-oz. pkg. frozen corn
salt and pepper to taste

Line the bottom of an ungreased 3-quart casserole dish with 4 bacon slices. Layer with lima beans, half the tomatoes, onion, green pepper, corn and remaining tomatoes. Sprinkle generously between layers with salt and pepper. Arrange remaining bacon slices on top. Cover and bake at 350 degrees for 1-1/2 hours, or until lima beans are tender. Uncover for the final 10 minutes to allow bacon to become crisp. Serves 8.

Make whimsical family placecards! Take lots of pictures of autumn fun...football games, hayrides, raking leaves and trick-or-treating. Then make color copies, cut out and glue to pieces of cardboard cut the same size.

Caesar Green Beans

Karen Boehme
Greensburg, PA

This zippy side dish is on our menu year 'round...it tastes
just as good cold, so it makes a great picnic food too!

18-oz. pkg. frozen cut
  green beans
2 T. oil
1 T. vinegar
1 T. dried, minced onion
1 clove garlic, crushed
1/4 t. salt

1/8 t. pepper
2 T. dry bread crumbs
2 T. grated Parmesan or Romano
  cheese
1 T. butter, melted
Garnish: paprika

Cook beans according to package directions; drain. Toss beans with oil, vinegar, onion, garlic, salt and pepper. Pour into a greased one-quart casserole dish. Toss together bread crumbs, cheese and melted butter; sprinkle over beans. Garnish with a little paprika. Bake, uncovered, at 350 degrees until heated through, about 15 to 20 minutes. Serve warm or chilled. Serves 4 to 6.

Barbecue Green Beans

Jennifer Breeden
Chesterfield, VA

My grandmother's recipe...it's one of the many ways we keep
Grandma's memory alive in our hearts. Mom often made
these beans and I've always loved them.

4 slices bacon, diced
1/4 c. onion, chopped
1/2 c. catsup
1/4 c. brown sugar, packed

1 T. Worcestershire sauce
2 15-oz. cans green beans,
  drained

In a skillet over medium heat, cook bacon and onion until bacon is crisp; drain. Add catsup, brown sugar and Worcestershire sauce; simmer for 2 minutes. Place beans in a lightly greased one-quart casserole dish. Pour bacon mixture over beans; do not stir. Bake, uncovered, at 350 degrees for 20 minutes, or until hot and bubbly. Serves 6.

Sally's Broccoli Puff

Sally Roberts
Fort Wayne, IN

*My mom and my sister just love this dish...it's so yummy
I can eat a whole pan myself! It's easy to fix, yet we
make it mostly for special occasions together.*

10-oz. pkg. frozen chopped
    broccoli
10-3/4 oz. can cream of
    mushroom soup
1/2 c. shredded sharp Cheddar
    cheese

1/4 c. milk
1/4 c. mayonnaise-style
    salad dressing
1 egg, beaten
1/4 c. dry bread crumbs
1 T. butter, melted

Cook broccoli according to package directions, omitting salt; drain.
Place in a lightly greased 10"x6" baking pan; set aside. In a bowl,
mix soup and cheese. Add milk, salad dressing and egg to soup
mixture; stir until well blended. Spoon over broccoli. Toss bread
crumbs with melted butter; sprinkle evenly over top. Bake, uncovered,
at 350 degrees for 45 minutes, or until lightly golden. Makes 6 to
8 servings.

Greet visitors with an oh-so-simple harvest decoration
that will last from Halloween to Thanksgiving. Roll out
an old wheelbarrow and heap it full of large,
colorful pumpkins and squash.

Caraway Pot Roast

Joan White
Malvern, PA

One of my favorite fall dinners...pure comfort food.

3-lb. boneless beef chuck roast
2 T. oil
2 onions, sliced
4 carrots, peeled and cut into
    chunks
1-1/4 c. apple cider
1 T. caraway seed

2 cloves garlic, minced
3/4 t. salt, divided
1/2 t. pepper, divided
2 T. cornstarch
1/4 c. cold water
1/2 c. sour cream

In a Dutch oven over medium-high heat, brown roast in oil on all sides; drain. In a bowl, combine onions, carrots, cider, caraway seed, garlic, 1/2 teaspoon salt and 1/4 teaspoon pepper. Pour mixture over roast. Bring to a boil. Reduce heat to low; cover and simmer for 3 to 3-1/2 hours, until roast is tender. Remove roast and vegetables to a platter; keep warm. Combine cornstarch and cold water in a small jar; shake until smooth. Stir cornstarch mixture into drippings in Dutch oven; cook and stir 2 minutes, or until thickened. Remove from heat; stir in sour cream and remaining salt and pepper. Serve sour cream mixture over sliced roast and vegetables. Makes 6 to 8 servings.

Get everyone outdoors for a little fresh air after Thanksgiving dinner...try pumpkin bowling! Simply roll pumpkins toward two-liter bottles filled with water. Sure to be a hit with kids of all ages!

Orange & Honey Yams
Vickie

*You'll love the scrumptious flavor of these sweet potatoes...
and you'll never miss the marshmallows!*

4 sweet potatoes, peeled and
   quartered
3 T. butter, softened
3 T. honey

1/4 c. orange juice
1/4 t. cayenne pepper
salt and pepper to taste

Place sweet potatoes in a lightly greased 13"x9" baking pan; set aside.
Melt butter in a small saucepan over low heat. Whisk in honey, orange
juice and cayenne pepper. Drizzle mixture over sweet potatoes; turn
to coat well and season with salt and pepper. Bake, uncovered, at
400 degrees for 45 to 55 minutes, stirring and basting occasionally
with pan juices. Serves 4.

One of my favorite memories of my mom is getting up early with
her on Thanksgiving morning to help her cook and watch the
Macy's Thanksgiving Day Parade. It was my job to help Mom
make the stuffing. She always told me, "The secret to good
stuffing is getting your hands in there and mixing it up."
I would stand by her side as she said, "More sage, more salt,
a li'l more pepper," then finally, "Perfect!" Then we'd stuff the
bird and butter him down. All this was orchestrated to the sound
of marching bands and celebrity announcers on the TV in the
background. Whenever I smell sage, I am sent straight back
to Thanksgiving mornings of my childhood.

–Beth Cassinos, Winnemucca, NV

Turkey Croquettes

Amy Wrightsel
Louisville, KY

My granny used to make these croquettes for me when I was a kid. They tasted so good fresh out of the fryer! Now my boys enjoy the croquettes too, and even tell their friends about them. It's a great recipe for using what's left of the Thanksgiving turkey.

6 T. butter
1/2 c. all-purpose flour
1 c. milk
1 c. chicken broth
2 t. lemon juice
2 T. fresh parsley, snipped
2 t. onion, grated
1/2 t. celery salt
1/8 t. pepper

1/8 t. paprika
1/8 t. nutmeg
4 c. cooked turkey, ground or
    finely chopped
3/4 c. dry bread crumbs
2 eggs, beaten
2 T. water
1 c. all-purpose flour
oil for deep frying

Melt butter in a large saucepan over low heat; blend in flour. Add milk and chicken broth. Cook and stir until mixture thickens and bubbles; continue cooking for one minute more. Add lemon juice, parsley, onion and seasonings; cool. In a large bowl, combine butter mixture with turkey; cover and chill thoroughly, one to 2 hours. Place bread crumbs in a shallow dish; whisk together eggs and water in a separate dish. With moistened hands, form turkey mixture into 2-inch balls. Roll balls in bread crumbs; lightly form into cone-shaped croquettes. Roll each croquette in flour; dip in egg mixture and roll in bread crumbs. Repeat so croquettes are double breaded. In a deep fryer or skillet over high heat, heat 4 inches oil to 375 degrees. Fry croquettes, a few at a time, turning until golden on all sides. Drain on paper towels. Serves 4.

Yummy finger foods call for lots of paper napkins. Dress up plain napkins in a jiffy with a large turkey rubber stamp and a colorful stamp pad... oh-so festive!

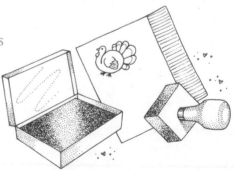

~~Thanksgiving with~~ All the Trimmings

Hazel's Stuffing Balls

Andrea Barclay
Somerset, PA

My mother-in-law gave me this recipe when I hosted my first Thanksgiving dinner. I have since learned that you have to take the bag of "goodies" out of the turkey before you roast it! Nowadays I usually double the recipe...you can't have too many stuffing balls! If you prefer, this stuffing can be used to stuff the turkey.

1-1/2 to 2 loaves white bread,
  torn into pieces
1/2 c. butter
1-1/2 to 2 c. celery, finely
  chopped
Optional: 1/2 c. onion, chopped
1-1/2 t. salt

1-1/2 t. pepper
1/2 t. poultry seasoning
1 to 2 t. dried parsley
6 eggs, beaten
1/4 to 1/2 c. turkey or chicken
  broth

The night before, place bread pieces on a baking sheet or in a large bowl to dry. The next day, melt butter in a skillet over medium-low heat. Sauté celery and onion, if using, for 15 to 20 minutes; cool slightly. In a very large bowl, toss bread pieces and seasonings with butter mixture. Add eggs and just enough broth to help mixture to stick together; mix well. Form into 12 balls; place in a 13"x9" baking pan sprayed with non-stick vegetable spray. Drizzle a little more broth over stuffing balls; cover with aluminum foil. Bake at 350 degrees for 20 to 30 minutes, uncovering for the last few minutes, until balls are crisp and golden. Serves 12.

Let the children help out with the Thanksgiving feast.
Something as simple as folding the napkins and setting
the table means time spent together, making memories.

Arugula Salad & Baked Pears
Sonya Labbe
West Hollywood, CA

This is a beautiful sweet and savory salad...my whole family loves it! Be sure to choose firm ripe pears.

3 Anjou pears, peeled and
   halved lengthwise
5 T. lemon juice
6 T. crumbled Gorgonzola
   cheese
1/4 c. sweetened dried cherries

1/4 c. pecan halves, toasted and
   chopped
1/2 c. apple cider
1/3 c. light brown sugar, packed
6-oz. pkg. arugula leaves
salt to taste

Core each pear half with a melon baller and a paring knife, creating a well. Trim bottoms of pear halves to sit flat. Drizzle pears with lemon juice and arrange, cored-side up, in an ungreased 8"x8" baking pan. In a small bowl, gently toss cheese, cherries and pecans together. Divide cheese mixture among pears, mounding it in the wells. In the same bowl, combine cider and brown sugar; stir to dissolve sugar. Pour cider mixture over and around pears. Bake, uncovered, at 375 degrees for 30 minutes, or until pears are tender, basting occasionally with cider mixture. Remove from oven, reserving cider mixture in pan; let stand until pears are warm or at room temperature. In a large bowl, add arugula to Dressing; toss well. Divide arugula mixture among 6 salad plates; top each with a pear half. Drizzle pears with some of the reserved cider mixture; sprinkle with salt and serve. Makes 6 servings.

Dressing:

1/4 c. olive oil
1/4 c. lemon juice

1/4 c. reserved cider mixture

Whisk together ingredients.

For a clever porch display, carve your house number into a pumpkin. Set it on the front steps and slip a lighted votive inside.

Almond-Orange Salad

Becky Butler
Keller, TX

A friend brought this salad to a potluck at work. I liked it so much that I ate some more for dessert! It's simple to make, but an appealing mix of flavors and textures. It's a terrific salad for winter, since oranges and romaine lettuce are readily available.

3 heads romaine, chopped
2 oranges, peeled and sectioned
1/2 c. slivered almonds, lightly toasted

In a large bowl, toss lettuce and orange segments together. Add most of Dressing to salad, tossing lightly to coat. Add almonds; toss lightly again. Serve immediately. Makes 8 to 10 servings.

Dressing:

3/4 c. olive oil
1/3 c. cider vinegar
2 T. orange juice
1/2 t. Dijon mustard
3/4 t. kosher salt, or to taste
1/2 t. pepper, or to taste
1/4 t. almond extract

Combine ingredients in a jar with a lid; shake well to mix. Refrigerate leftovers.

Be sure to have lots of comfy pillows and piles of cozy blankets on hand for early-morning parade watchers and after-dinner nappers!

Cranberry Fruit Conserve

Ruby Dickson
McAlester, OK

This recipe was my mother's. I loved this festive dish when I was little, and I'm so glad I have her recipe.

12-oz. pkg. fresh cranberries
1-3/4 c. sugar
1 c. water
1 Granny Smith apple, peeled,
    cored and chopped

zest and juice of 1 orange
zest and juice of 1 lemon
3/4 c. raisins
3/4 c. chopped walnuts or
    pecans

In a saucepan, combine cranberries, sugar and water. Cook over low heat for 5 minutes, or until cranberries pop. Add apple, citrus zest and juice; continue cooking for 15 minutes. Remove from heat; stir in raisins and nuts. Cover and refrigerate; serve chilled. Makes 4 servings.

Honey-Orange Butter

Jill Ball
Highland, UT

I love to give something homemade and personal as gifts. This recipe has become one of my favorites for giving with a loaf of bread.

1/2 c. butter, softened
1/4 c. honey

2 T. orange juice
1 T. orange zest

In a small bowl, blend all ingredients until smooth. Cover and refrigerate for at least 2 hours. Bring to room temperature before serving. Makes one cup.

Spoon homemade jams and spreads into pretty crocks or vintage blue canning jars for hostess gifts. Tie on a vintage silver spreader and a recipe card...sure to be appreciated!

Spirited Cherry Salad

Cathy Hillier
Salt Lake City, UT

Whenever we went to Grandmother's for Thanksgiving and Christmas dinner, we knew this shimmery gelatin salad would be on the menu. I still love it!

16-oz. can dark sweet cherries, drained and juice reserved
3-oz. pkg. cherry gelatin mix
3/4 c. red port wine or grape juice
1/2 c. chopped almonds
Garnish: lettuce leaves, mayonnaise-style salad dressing

Pour reserved cherry juice into a 2-cup glass measuring cup. Add enough water to equal 1-1/4 cups. Pour into a saucepan; bring to a boil over medium heat. Place dry gelatin mix in a bowl; pour hot juice mixture over top and stir to dissolve. Let cool slightly; stir in wine or grape juice, cherries and almonds. Pour into a 1-1/2 quart gelatin mold; cover and chill until set. At serving time, unmold salad. Serve portions on lettuce-lined salad plates, garnished with dollops of salad dressing. Makes 6 to 8 servings.

Molded gelatin salads were everywhere in the 1950s, and they're still a refreshing make-ahead dish. Vintage copper molds can often be found at flea markets...dress up a kitchen wall with a whimsical display.

Crunchy Turkey Casserole

Lori Patterson
Manitoba, Canada

The first time I made this dish with its crispy topping,
my husband declared it was his #1 favorite dish.
After more than ten years, it's still his all-time favorite!

10-3/4 oz. cream of chicken
  soup
3/4 c. mayonnaise
1 T. onion, minced
3/4 c. celery, diced
3 c. cooked turkey, diced

1 c. sliced mushrooms
1/2 c. slivered almonds
Optional: 1/2 c. sliced black
  olives
1-1/2 c. chow mein noodles,
  crushed

In a large bowl, combine soup, mayonnaise and onion; stir to mix
well and set aside. Place celery in a microwave-safe bowl; microwave
on high for 1-1/2 minutes, until partially cooked. Add celery, turkey,
mushrooms, almonds and olives, if using, to soup mixture. Mix
thoroughly. Transfer to a lightly greased 3-quart casserole dish.
Sprinkle chow mein noodles on top. Bake, uncovered, at 350 degrees
for 30 minutes, or until heated through. Makes 8 servings.

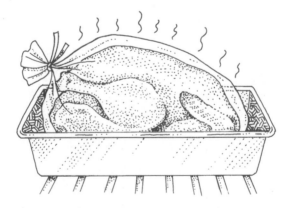

Shopping for a turkey? Allow about one pound per person
plus a little extra for leftovers. For example, a 15-pound turkey
would serve 12 people with enough left to enjoy turkey
sandwiches, turkey tetrazzini or turkey soup later.

Delicious Creamed Turkey

Nancy Weiford
Buena Park, CA

The day after Thanksgiving, when my family still wants turkey,
but with a new twist, I serve this casserole with a carrot &
pineapple-orange gelatin salad...it's always a hit!

3 c. cooked turkey, diced
1/2 c. celery, diced
1/4 c. onion, diced
1 c. peas
1 c. corn
1/2 c. mushrooms, chopped
1/2 c. slivered almonds
1 t. dill weed
1 t. dried thyme
1 t. dried parsley
1 t. dried basil

1/2 t. salt
1/2 t. pepper
2 c. whipping cream
1/2 c. water, divided
1 c. shredded Cheddar cheese
Optional: 1 to 4 t. cornstarch
6 English muffins, split and
 toasted, or 6 puff pastry
 shells, baked
Garnish: melted butter
Optional: capers

In a large saucepan over low heat, combine turkey, vegetables, mushrooms, almonds and seasonings. Add just enough water to cover ingredients by 1/2 inch. Simmer, watching closely, until vegetables are tender and most of water is evaporated. Add cream and 1/2 cup water. Continue to simmer, stirring constantly. Gently stir in cheese. Add cornstarch, one teaspoon at a time, if needed to thicken to desired consistency. Simmer over medium heat for 15 minutes. Serve over English muffin halves or puff pastry shells brushed with butter. Garnish with capers, if desired. Serves 6.

When returning Grandma's good china plates to
the cupboard, slip a paper plate between each to
keep the china from becoming scratched.

Family-Favorite Mac & Cheese   *Julie Remer*
Gahanna, OH

*This is a revised version of the macaroni & cheese my mom made
for us when we were growing up. She learned how to make it
in her high school Home Ec class...now I make it for my kids!*

16-oz. pkg. elbow macaroni,
   uncooked
1 egg
1/2 c. butter, divided
1/4 c. all-purpose flour
2-1/2 c. skim milk
2 t. dry mustard

16-oz. pkg. shredded Cheddar
   cheese, divided
1/2 t. seasoned salt
1/2 t. salt
1/2 t. pepper
1-1/2 c. soft bread crumbs,
   divided

Cook macaroni according to package directions; drain and set aside.
Meanwhile, beat egg in a medium bowl and set aside. In a large
saucepan, melt 1/4 cup butter over medium-low heat. Add flour and
cook, whisking constantly, for 5 minutes. Add milk and mustard;
whisk until smooth. Continue to cook and whisk until sauce is very
thick, 5 to 8 minutes. Reduce heat to low. Remove 1/4 cup of hot milk
mixture and slowly add it to the egg, whisking until combined. Pour
this mixture back into the saucepan and stir. Set aside 1/2 cup cheese
for topping. Add remaining cheese to mixture in saucepan; stir until
completely melted. Stir in seasonings and macaroni. Melt remaining
butter; toss with bread crumbs. Sprinkle half of crumb mixture into a
greased 3-quart casserole dish; spoon in macaroni mixture. Top with
remaining crumb mixture and cheese. Cover and bake at 350 degrees
for 20 to 25 minutes, until bubbly and golden. Serves 8.

For a bountiful display on
the Thanksgiving buffet, serve
fresh-baked dinner rolls, muffins
and scones tumbling out of
a wicker cornucopia basket.

Parmesan Potatoes

Gretchen Mortlock
Vancouver, WA

I often make these savory potatoes when we have
guests for dinner...they're always enjoyed!

5 lbs. russet potatoes, peeled
   and sliced 1/4-inch thick
3 t. salt, divided
1/2 t. pepper
1-1/2 T. fresh rosemary, minced

3/4 c. crumbled blue cheese
1-1/2 c. shredded Parmesan
   cheese, divided
1 c. sour cream
2 c. whipping cream

In a large bowl, toss potatoes with 2 teaspoons salt, pepper and rosemary. Layer half of the potatoes in a buttered 13"x9" baking pan. In a small bowl, toss blue cheese and 3/4 cup Parmesan cheese together. Sprinkle half of cheese mixture over potatoes. In a separate bowl, whisk together sour cream, whipping cream and remaining salt. Pour cream mixture over potatoes. Tap baking pan gently to release any air bubbles. Sprinkle with remaining cheese mixture; top with remaining Parmesan cheese. Bake, uncovered, at 350 degrees for one hour and 30 minutes, or until golden and potatoes are tender. Makes 8 servings.

Make a nostalgic garland for the mantel...snip photos of family, friends, pets, anything you're thankful for. Clipped to a ribbon with mini clothespins, they're a heartfelt reminder to count your blessings.

Crunchy Cashew Slaw

Lori Comer
Kernersville, NC

A dear friend brought this salad to our Sunday School dinner
after church...every lady there wanted the recipe!
It's scrumptious and so simple to make.

16-oz. pkg. coleslaw mix
2 3-oz. pkgs. chicken-flavored
   ramen noodles
1/2 c. sugar

1/3 c. vinegar
1/4 c. oil
1 c. cashew halves
1 c. sunflower seeds

Place coleslaw mix in a large salad bowl. Crush noodles and add to coleslaw, setting aside seasoning packets; toss to mix. In a separate small bowl, whisk together sugar, vinegar, oil and reserved seasoning; pour over coleslaw mixture. Toss again; cover and chill 2 hours. Do not chill overnight as the noodles will become soggy. At serving time, add cashew halves and sunflower seeds. Mix well and serve. Makes 10 to 12 servings.

Transfer gilded imprints of fall foliage onto plain cotton napkins in no time. Using a foam brush, apply a little gold craft paint to the backs of collected oak, maple or sycamore leaves and press away...just right for autumn meals!

Thanksgiving with All the Trimmings

Sandra's Pomegranate Salad

Sandra Smith
Lancaster, CA

Here in California, people have pomegranate trees in their yards, and we had three such trees at our old house. I also make pomegranate jelly and a pomegranate cordial, but this salad is a favorite.

2 bunches arugula, torn
2 ripe pears, halved, cored and
   cut into wedges
2 T. lime juice
2 T. olive oil
1/2 t. Dijon mustard
salt and pepper to taste

seeds of 1 pomegranate
Optional: 1/2 c. crumbled
   feta cheese, 1/3 c. toasted
   chopped pecans
Garnish: Boston or Bibb lettuce
   leaves

Place arugula and pears in a large salad bowl; set aside. In a small bowl, whisk together lime juice, olive oil and mustard. Toss arugula and pears with just enough lime juice mixture to coat; season with salt and pepper. Sprinkle salad with pomegranate seeds; add cheese and pecans, if using. Line 6 salad plates with lettuce leaves; place a serving of salad in the center of each. Serves 6.

Pick up a new-to-you fall fruit like quince, persimmon or pomegranate at a farmstand. Ask the vendor how to prepare them...he or she is sure to have some tasty suggestions to share!

Aunt Patty's Pea Salad

Jodi Griggs
Richmond, KY

Whenever our extended family gets together, we all beg
Aunt Patty to bring her salad...it's a real favorite!

15-oz. can baby peas, drained
15-oz. can shoepeg corn,
   drained
14-1/2 oz. can French-style
   green beans, drained
14-1/2 oz. can lima beans,
   drained

2-oz. jar chopped pimentos,
   drained
1 c. red onion, chopped
1 c. green pepper, chopped
1 c. celery, chopped

In a large salad bowl, mix together all ingredients. Drizzle with Salad Dressing; toss to mix. For the best flavor, cover and refrigerate at least 8 hours to overnight. Serves 8.

Salad Dressing:

3/4 c. white vinegar
1/2 c. oil

3/4 c. sugar
salt and pepper to taste

In a small bowl, whisk together all ingredients.

Create a beautiful fall centerpiece in a snap! Hot-glue brightly colored ears of mini Indian corn around a terra-cotta pot and set a vase of orange or yellow mums in the center.

Broccoli Salad Supreme

Billie Jean Elliott
Woodsfield, OH

This recipe was shared by a friend and it makes the best-ever salad. Broccoli is one of those green veggies we should all eat more of...this salad makes it easy!

1 bunch broccoli, finely chopped
1 onion, finely chopped
1 c. celery, finely chopped
1/2 c. raisins, finely chopped
1/2 to 1 lb. bacon, crisply cooked and crumbled

1/4 c. mayonnaise
1/4 c. sugar
2 T. vinegar
1-1/2 t. mustard
1 c. shredded Colby cheese

In a large bowl, combine broccoli, onion, celery, raisins and bacon; toss to mix and set aside. In a separate small bowl, mix mayonnaise, sugar, vinegar and mustard. Pour mayonnaise mixture over broccoli mixture; stir gently. Cover and refrigerate at least 4 hours to overnight. Top with cheese just before serving. Serves 6 to 8.

As a child, I lived with my grandparents on their Kansas farm. Our harvest was amber waves of grain, wheat! Every harvest time, I got to help Grandma cook and pack up her three or four-course hot meals to take to the fields for the workers...fried chicken, salads, dessert, jugs of cool water or iced tea. I thought my grandma was the luckiest woman in the world to have a picnic everyday...sometimes twice a day! Can you imagine how much fun she was having? When I was older, with children, I realized I was the lucky one. Lucky because I had such a strong role model in my life. I learned quite young how to provide for my family. Thanks, Grandma!

—Rita Jefferis, Anthony, KS

Cranberry Orchard Salad

Cindy Wetzig
Belleville, IL

My mother-in-law Jo always made this salad for Thanksgiving and she gave me the recipe. I've been making it for our family for nearly 25 years and it's still a favorite. We enjoy it with our Christmas prime rib dinner too. It's easy to make ahead, the day before...one less thing to do on Thanksgiving or Christmas Day!

1-1/2 c. fresh cranberries
1/2 c. sugar
6-oz. pkg. orange gelatin mix
1/4 t. salt
2 c. boiling water
1-1/2 c. cold water
1 T. lemon juice
1/4 t. cinnamon

1/8 t. ground cloves
1 orange or 2 clementines,
   peeled, sectioned and diced
1/2 c. chopped walnuts
Garnish: whole cranberries,
   fresh parsley sprigs or
   orange segments

Process cranberries in a food processor until finely ground. Combine cranberries and sugar in a bowl; set aside. In a separate large bowl, dissolve dry gelatin mix and salt in boiling water. Stir in cold water, lemon juice and spices. Cover and refrigerate until partially thickened, one to 1-1/2 hours. Fold in cranberry mixture, oranges or clementines and nuts; spoon into a 6-cup mold. Cover and chill until firm, about 4 hours. Unmold onto a serving platter; garnish as desired. Makes 12 servings.

Candied cranberries are a lovely garnish. In a saucepan, bring one cup water and one cup sugar almost to a boil, stirring until sugar dissolves. Pour into a bowl and add one cup fresh cranberries; chill overnight. Drain cranberries well. Toss with superfine sugar to coat and dry on wax paper.

Festive Fall Flavors

Cranberry Chicken Spread

Patrice Lindsey
Lockport, IL

When I took this quick and tasty spread to a party, it was a huge hit! It also makes a nice luncheon salad served on a bed of lettuce. Save time by using rotisserie chicken or canned chicken.

1-3/4 c. cooked chicken, finely chopped
1 c. walnuts, finely chopped
2/3 c. mayonnaise
1 stalk celery, finely chopped
1 onion, finely chopped
1/2 to 1 t. salt
1/2 t. garlic powder
1/2 c. sweetened dried cranberries, chopped
assorted crackers

In a bowl, combine all ingredients except crackers; mix well. Cover and chill 3 to 4 hours, to allow flavors to blend. Serve with assorted crackers. Makes about 3 cups.

When my children were growing up, my husband, father and brothers were members of a hunting club. On Sunday afternoons every fall, the family would gather at the camp to have a picnic, roast hot dogs and make s'mores over the open fire. The kids played simple, fun games, hiked in the woods and we all just enjoyed each other's company. Times have changed, but the kids, all grown with children of their own, still talk about those days in the woods. The simple things really are the best!

–Ann Brandau, Cheboygan, MI

Festive Fall Flavors

Pineapple Cheese Ball

Julie Ann Perkins
Anderson, IN

This is one of my family's favorite cheese balls! We make it for holidays and birthdays...it's also a must on football nights.

2 8-oz. pkgs. cream cheese,
   softened
8-oz. can pineapple tidbits,
   drained
2 to 4 T. onion, chopped
1/2 c. green pepper, chopped

1/2 t. salt
Optional: pepper to taste
2 c. chopped pecans or walnuts
snack crackers, pita wedges and
   celery sticks

In a bowl, blend together cream cheese, pineapple, onion, green pepper and seasonings. Mix well; roll into one or 2 balls. Roll in chopped nuts to coat. Wrap in plastic wrap; keep refrigerated. Serve with crackers, pita wedges and celery. Serves 10 to 15.

For no-stress entertaining, have an all-appetizers party!
Set up tables in different areas so guests can mingle as they
enjoy yummy spreads and finger foods. Your get-together
is sure to be a scrumptious success.

Mini Corn Quiches

Deborah Patterson
Carmichael, CA

On beautiful fall evenings, I love to sit on my patio and enjoy these little treats with my family. No need to spend a lot of time in the kitchen cooking!

2 9-inch pie crusts
12-oz. pkg. frozen corn soufflé
1/3 c. cooked ham, diced
1/4 c. sour cream
1 egg, lightly beaten
2 T. green onion, chopped

1 T. all-purpose flour
1/8 t. pepper
3/4 c. shredded Swiss cheese,
   divided
Garnish: sliced green onion,
   diced red pepper

Roll out one pie crust on a lightly floured surface; cut into 18, 2-inch squares. Repeat with remaining crust, totaling 36 squares. Press each crust square into a well-greased mini muffin cup; set aside. Microwave soufflé on 50% power for 6 to 7 minutes, until thawed. In a bowl, stir together soufflé, ham, sour cream, egg, onion, flour, pepper and 1/2 cup cheese. Fill muffin cups 3/4 cup full; sprinkle with remaining cheese. Bake at 375 degrees for 30 to 35 minutes, until crust and filling are golden. Cool in muffin tins on wire racks for 5 minutes. Top with garnish. Makes 3 dozen.

Burlap fabric makes a terrific no-sew rustic tablecloth...
wonderful for harvest-time gatherings. To fringe the ends,
just pull away threads, one row at a time.

Festive Fall Flavors

Seasoned Spinach Balls

Donna Williams
Bartlett, TN

Everyone loves these savory bite-size appetizers!

2 10-oz. pkgs frozen chopped
   spinach, thawed and well
   drained
2 c. herb-flavored stuffing mix,
   crushed

1 c. grated Parmesan cheese
4 eggs, lightly beaten
3/4 c. margarine, softened
1/2 c. onion, finely chopped

Combine all ingredients in a large bowl; mix well. Form into one-inch balls; arrange on ungreased baking sheets. Bake at 350 degrees for 10 to 12 minutes, until set. Makes about 2 dozen.

Back in the early 1960s, I grew up in a very old-fashioned neighborhood with a barber shop, a beauty shop and a little store where we bought penny candy. Every Halloween, my sister Peggy and I put on our costumes and went trick-or-treating with our girlfriends. Our house was always a popular stop for the trick-or-treaters. Dad was a milkman and he went to a local distributor to buy boxes of candy bars to give out...full-size candy bars, not little bite-size bars! At one of our favorite stops, a old lady always gave us freshly made doughnuts...yum! We could never quite make it home without taking a bite first. Candle-lit Jack-o'-Lanterns still bring back cozy memories of a time when you knew everything was right in the world.

–Denise Hamilton, Springfield, OH

Firehouse Hot Meatballs

Lea Burwell
Charles Town, WV

A friend who's a fireman gave me this slow-cooker recipe. It's popular at the firehouse because they can just put it all together and forget it. When the fireman got back from a call it would be waiting and could even become a whole dinner if served over rice. These meatballs aren't too hot...they just have a little kick!

40-oz. pkg. frozen meatballs
2 15-oz. bottles hot & spicy
   catsup

2-ltr. bottle ginger ale

Place frozen meatballs in a slow cooker; pour both bottles of catsup over top. Add enough ginger ale to cover meatballs. Cover and cook on high setting for one hour. Turn setting to low; cook an additional 3 to 4 hours. Stir before serving. Makes about 6-1/2 dozen.

Dress up stemmed glasses in a jiffy. Cut or tear fabric into
1/2-inch wide strips and tie a length around the stem of
the glass. Choose team colors for game-day parties,
harvest shades for Thanksgiving...the sky's the limit!

Festive Fall Flavors

Sneaky-Good Sausages

Tammy Mahoney
Sarasota, FL

I used to make these yummy appetizers for our church dinners. My girlfriend's two sons would sneak down to the basement to hide the slow cooker, then eat them all before anyone else even got any. When she scolded them, they always said, "But gee, Mom, they're so good!" Yummy served over noodles, mashed potatoes or rice too.

4 4-oz. jars puréed apricot
    baby food
1 c. brown sugar, packed

3 14-oz. pkgs. mini smoked
    sausages

Stir together baby food and brown sugar in a slow cooker. Cut each sausage into 4 pieces; add to slow cooker and stir again. Cover and cook on low setting for 4 hours. Makes about 11 dozen.

Maple-Glazed Frankies

The Loomis Barn
Rushville, NY

At our shop, we offered samples of this recipe to shoppers during our Maple Weekend...it was a hit!

1 T. butter, sliced
1 T. soy sauce

1/4 c. pure maple syrup
14-oz. pkg. cocktail wieners

In a saucepan over medium-low heat, stir together butter, soy sauce and maple syrup until slightly thickened. Add wieners and heat through. Makes about 3-1/2 dozen.

Turn the plainest food into a feast with festive trimmings. Pick up napkins and table coverings in team colors at the nearest dollar store and you're halfway to a tailgating party!

Curried Chicken Party Rolls

Tracee Cummins
Amarillo, TX

This is a great recipe for any party! It's dainty enough for showers yet hearty enough for tailgating. The filling can be made ahead of time and spooned into the rolls just before serving. For a terrific buffet tray, vary the types of dinner rolls...wheat, pumpernickel and sourdough all go well with the curry-flavored filling.

1/2 c. mayonnaise or
    mayonnaise-style
    salad dressing
1/4 c. orange marmalade
2 t. curry powder

2 c. cooked chicken, chopped
1/2 c. golden raisins
1/4 c. green onions, sliced
1/4 c. slivered almonds, toasted
1 doz. dinner rolls

Mix mayonnaise or salad dressing, marmalade and curry powder in a large bowl. Add remaining ingredients except rolls; mix lightly. Cover and chill. Slice off tops of rolls and scoop out centers, being careful not to tear through the crust. Spoon chicken salad into prepared rolls; replace tops. Arrange rolls on a serving platter; cover and refrigerate until serving time. Makes 12 servings.

For Indian Summer get-togethers, serve up appetizers outside on the porch or deck. Arrange hay bales for casual seating, light tables with tealights placed in hollowed-out apples and fill sap buckets with sprays of bittersweet. Sure to be memorable!

Festive Fall Flavors

Very Best Veggie Cheese

Cathy Daniels
Miamisburg, OH

I have no idea where I found this recipe, but it has become my go-to recipe for parties. One time I made it as a spread for bagels and saw a lady fill a plate, cover it with another plate and tuck it in her handbag...that's how good it is!

8-oz. pkg. cream cheese,
   softened
1/2 c. finely shredded Cheddar
   cheese
1/4 c. finely shredded Parmesan
   cheese
1/4 c. cucumber, finely chopped
1/4 c. green pepper, finely
   chopped
1/4 c. celery, finely chopped
1/4 c. zucchini, finely chopped
1/4 c. carrot, peeled and finely
   chopped
1 t. onion powder
1 t. garlic powder
hot pepper sauce to taste
pretzel crisps, crackers or sliced
   bagels

In a large bowl, blend cheeses together. Add vegetables; stir well. Add seasonings and hot pepper sauce; mix well. Add more hot sauce, if desired. Chill and serve with pretzel crisps, crackers or bagels. Makes 1-1/2 cups.

Keep food in coolers fresh and cool with homemade ice packs. In a gallon-size plastic zipping bag, combine 2 cups water, one cup rubbing alcohol and 2 to 3 drops blue food coloring. Seal very well, leaving room for expansion, and freeze. Bags may be refrozen and re-used several times.

Game-Day Bacon-Nut Mix

Paula Marchesi
Lenhartsville, PA

I love football! I make all kinds of snacks and place them on a large table by our big-screen TV. This way, everyone can help themselves without missing a minute of the action. This nut mixture is everyone's favorite...I'm sure you'll love it too!

1 lb. bacon, diced
1/3 c. brown sugar, packed
16-oz. pkg. pecan halves
16-oz. pkg. walnut halves
16-oz. pkg. honey-roasted
   peanuts

16-oz. pkg. salted cashews
4 t. Italian seasoning
4 t. sugar
1 t. kosher salt
1 t. cayenne pepper
2 t. olive oil

In a skillet over medium heat, cook bacon until crisp. Drain bacon on paper towels, discarding drippings. Return bacon to skillet; add brown sugar. Cook over medium heat, stirring to coat bacon, until crisp and caramelized, about 3 minutes. Watch carefully to avoid burning. Remove from heat; set aside. Spread nuts on a baking sheet lined with parchment paper. Bake at 350 degrees until warm, about 5 minutes. In a very large bowl, combine remaining ingredients. Add nuts and toss until well coated. Stir in bacon mixture. Cool; store in an airtight container. Makes about 17 cups.

Slip harvest-party invitations into fabric bags that can do double duty...they can be used later to hold Halloween treats!

Festive Fall
Flavors

Game-Time Pretzels

Kristin Rentschler
Columbia City, IN

*My best friend Sarah always whips up a batch of these delicious
pretzels for our football parties...they're fantastic!*

2 16-oz. pkgs. Dutch sourdough
  pretzels
16-oz. bottle butter-flavored
  popcorn popping oil

1-oz. pkg. ranch salad dressing
  mix
1 T. dill weed
1 t. garlic powder

Break up pretzels into bite-size pieces; place in a large roasting pan.
In a separate bowl, mix together remaining ingredients. Drizzle
mixture onto pretzels and stir until pretzels are well coated. Bake at
250 degrees for one hour, stirring every 20 minutes. Spread pretzels
out on paper towels to cool. Store in an airtight container or a large
plastic zipping bag. Makes 10 to 12 servings.

For a tasty, almost-instant appetizer, set an unwrapped
block of cream cheese on a serving plate, spoon zesty salsa
over it and serve with crunchy corn chips.

Laurie's Famous Bruschetta
Laurie Anderson
Mount Prospect, IL

Everywhere I take this bruschetta, people just rave and ask for the recipe. Sometimes I add an extra clove or two of garlic, or use a mix of shredded Parmesan and Romano cheese for even more flavor. On the rare occasion that we have leftovers, we eat it right out of the bowl with a spoon...it's that good!

8 roma tomatoes, diced
5 green onions, chopped
3 to 4 cloves garlic, minced
1 T. fresh basil, chopped
1/3 c. olive oil
2 t. dried oregano
1 t. dried parsley

1 t. salt
1/2 t. pepper
1/2 c. finely shredded Parmesan
   cheese
sliced French bread or baguette,
   or baked garlic snack toast

In a large bowl, combine all ingredients except cheese and bread or toast; toss gently. Cover and chill at least one hour. At serving time, add cheese and lightly toss again. Serve on slices of bread or toast. Makes about 3-1/2 cups.

Show your spirit...dress up a garden scarecrow in
a hometown football jersey. Go team!

Festive Fall Flavors

Poor Man's Appetizer

Tracy Needham
San Tan Valley, AZ

This is the very first appetizer my mom taught me to make. It's suitable for any occasion and will please just about anyone.

1 c. mayonnaise
1/4 c. red onion, chopped

3 T. grated Parmesan cheese
1 baguette, sliced 1/4-inch thick

In a bowl, mix mayonnaise, onion and cheese. Spread mixture onto baguette slices; place on an ungreased baking sheet. Turn oven broiler to high with rack set 2 slots down. Broil until tops are golden and bubbly. Remove from baking sheet; allow to cool slightly before serving. Serves 6 to 8.

Couldn't-Be-Easier Tapenade

Tiffani Schulte
Wyandotte, MI

We love olives at our house, so I decided to try to come up with an olive tapenade recipe using the inexpensive black and pimento-stuffed green olives I always have on hand. The result was a hit! We often serve it over grilled chicken too.

6-oz. can black olives, drained
1 c. green olives with pimentos
1 clove garlic
3 T. olive oil
3 T. balsamic vinegar

1/2 t. salt
Optional: 1/2 c. fresh parsley,
    chopped
1 loaf French bread, sliced and
    toasted, or pita chips

In a food processor, combine all ingredients except bread slices or chips. Pulse lightly to desired spreading or dipping consistency. To serve, spread on toasted bread slices or scoop up with pita chips. Makes 12 servings.

Spoon hot tomato soup into a thermos and bring along to the high school football game...sure to take the chill right off!

Jim's Cheeseburger Bowl Dip
Carolyn Deckard
Bedford, IN

My husband Jim's specialty! This scrumptious warm appetizer is very popular at tailgating parties. Use ground turkey instead of beef, if you like.

2 16-oz. loaves Hawaiian-style
   bread
1 lb. ground beef
1 t. seasoning salt
1/2 t. pepper
1-1/2 lbs. pasteurized process
   cheese spread, cubed

7 slices bacon, crisply cooked
   and crumbled
1 c. tomatoes, diced
1/4 c. red onion, chopped
1/3 c. dill pickles, chopped
Optional: Thousand Island salad
   dressing

Hollow out the center of one loaf, keeping loaf intact and leaving 2 inches of bottom and sides. Cut reserved bread and remaining loaf into one-inch cubes for dipping; set aside. Brown beef in a skillet over medium heat; drain. Stir in seasonings to taste. Add cheese to beef; stir until melted. Add bacon and tomatoes; stir to mix well. Spoon warm mixture into hollowed-out bread bowl. Top with onion and pickles to taste. Drizzle with salad dressing, if desired. Surround bread bowl with bread cubes for dipping. Makes 8 to 10 servings.

Having a Halloween party? Tried & true games are fun
for all ages...bobbing for apples, telling ghost stories and
visiting the mad scientist's lab to touch cauliflower
"brains" and peeled grape "eyeballs."

Feisty Red Pepper-Bacon Dip
Andrea Heyart
Aubrey, TX

I like to make this dip for small gatherings and leisurely weekends at home. If there's any left over, I use it as a sandwich spread the next day for an unbeatable turkey sandwich!

1/2 c. cream cheese, softened
8-oz. container sour cream
1 T. creamy horseradish
7-oz. jar roasted red peppers,
   drained

4 to 5 slices bacon, crisply
   cooked and crumbled
Optional: additional crumbled
   bacon, minced fresh chives
snack crackers

Combine all ingredients except crackers in a large bowl. Beat with an electric mixer on low speed until mixed well. Cover and refrigerate for at least one hour. Garnish with additional crumbled bacon and chives, if desired. Serve with crackers. Makes about 2 cups.

Thanksgiving is so family-centered...why not host a post-holiday potluck with friends later in the weekend? Everyone can bring their favorite "leftover" concoctions, relax and catch up together.

Italian Hamburgers

Gladys Brehm
Quakertown, PA

This is a great quick & easy recipe for entertaining family & friends at cookouts. I have had several friends request it once they tasted my burgers. It's such a good feeling to be able to share your recipes with folks who enjoy your cooking!

2 to 3 slices bacon, crisply
    cooked and crumbled
3 lbs. ground beef
.7-oz. pkg. Italian salad dressing
    mix
2 eggs, beaten
1 c. Italian-flavored dry bread
    crumbs
1 c. shredded mozzarella cheese
12 to 14 hamburger buns, split

In a large bowl, combine all ingredients except buns. Mix well and form into 12 to 14 patties. Grill to preferred doneness. Serve on buns. Makes 12 to 14 servings.

Gridiron eggs! Make a platter of yummy deviled eggs, then top each egg with strips of pimento to resemble a football. Clever!

Mom's Chili Dogs

Catherine Sedosky
Charleston, WV

Here in West Virginia we like our hot dogs topped with everything! This chili sauce is a must at all of our family cookouts.

1 lb. lean ground beef	3 T. chili powder
1 onion, chopped	1 t. salt
1/2 c. catsup	Optional: 1 t. vinegar
6-oz. can tomato paste	10 to 12 hot dogs, cooked
2-1/4 c. water	10 to 12 hot dog buns

Combine all ingredients in a large stockpot over medium-high heat; do not brown beef. Stir well. Cover; bring to a boil. Reduce heat to low; simmer for 2 to 3 hours, stirring occasionally to break up beef. To serve, spoon over hot dogs in buns. Makes 10 to 12 servings.

Fall is homecoming time! Do you have an album full of old photos from school? Pull out all the funniest ones...slumber parties, proms and band camp. Make color copies and slip them into invitations for all your girlfriends. Enjoy coffee and desserts together...and a lot of laughs too!

Secret Sandwich for a Crowd

Tina Kerns
Hilliard, OH

This is always a huge Buckeye game-day hit! I like to use
rolled-out pizza dough from a local pizza shop instead of
the frozen bread loaves for convenience.

2 16-oz. loaves frozen bread
  dough, thawed
1 lb. hard salami, sliced and
  divided
1 lb. pepperoni, sliced and
  divided
1-1/2 lbs. deli ham, sliced and
  divided

1-1/4 lbs. provolone cheese,
  sliced and divided
2 eggs, beaten
1 t. salt
1/2 t. dried basil

Spread one loaf of thawed dough out on a lightly greased baking sheet.
Arrange slices of salami, pepperoni, ham and cheese over dough in
3 rows, using half of each ingredient. Fold over both long edges of
dough toward center; pinch seams to seal. In a small bowl, whisk eggs
with salt and basil; brush half of mixture lightly over top. Repeat with
remaining loaf and other ingredients on a second baking sheet. Bake
at 350 degrees for 30 minutes, until golden. Slice; serve warm. Makes
2 sandwiches, about 18 slices per sandwich.

Give pumpkins a glittery
sparkle...it's so easy. Lightly
coat the outside of a pumpkin
with spray adhesive and
dust with fine glitter; set aside
to dry. If time is short, use a
paintbrush to apply white glue
to the stem only, then dust it
with glitter. Try using purple
and lime green as well as
gold...beautiful!

Festive Fall Flavors

Spiced Pineapple Sparkle

Kerry Hoyle
Pollock Pines, CA

This delightful punch is a staple at family gatherings during the winter. A hot cup of it really warms you up after a day in the snow!

2/3 c. sugar
1-1/2 c. water
3 4-inch cinnamon sticks
12 whole cloves
46-oz. can pineapple juice

1-1/2 c. orange juice
1/2 c. lemon juice
28-oz. bottle ginger ale, room
  temperature

Combine sugar and water in a large saucepan. Add cinnamon sticks and cloves, wrapped and tied in cheesecloth, if desired. Cover and simmer over medium heat for 15 minutes. Discard spices; pour sugar mixture into a large heatproof pitcher. Stir in juices and ginger ale. Serve warm or chilled. Makes 8 to 10 servings.

For a fruit-studded ice ring that won't dilute your holiday punch, arrange sliced oranges, lemons and limes in a ring mold. Pour in a small amount of punch and freeze until set. Add enough punch to fill mold and freeze until solid. To turn out, dip mold carefully in warm water.

Cranberry BBQ Pork Rolls

Samantha Place
Wilmington, VT

Slow-cooking the pork makes it super tender, and it's so easy!
We like to use our favorite sweet onion barbecue sauce in this recipe.

2 to 3-lb. pork loin or roast
salt and pepper to taste
16-oz. can cranberry sauce
1/2 c. barbecue sauce

Optional: additional barbecue
   sauce
10 sandwich rolls, split

Trim most of the fat from pork. Sprinkle pork with salt and pepper; place in a slow cooker. Mix sauces together and spoon over pork. Cover and cook on low setting for 6 to 8 hours, until pork is very tender. Shred pork in slow cooker with 2 forks; add more barbecue sauce if needed. Cover and cook on low setting for another 20 to 30 minutes. Serve on rolls. Makes 10 servings.

As the weather turns cooler and the leaves start changing, we know it's time for our family's pine cone hunt. We started this tradition when our kids were young and it's carried out by our grandkids now. As we go in search of the best pine cones, it's wonderful to hear the children's laughter and excitement! The kids always see who can find the biggest pine cone, the best shape and so forth. Afterwards it's time for punch and cookies, then we make our fall baskets with pine cones, acorns, cinnamon sticks and a harvest ribbon. Wow! A family-made centerpiece to greet friends as they come into our home. For Christmas we spray the pine cones silver, gold, red or green and sprinkle them with glue and glitter. It's a lot of fun and hard to believe we started this tradition over 20 years ago. Such a simple thing that's become one of my favorites during the holiday season.

–Karen Hughes, Newberry, SC

Festive Fall
Flavors

Slow-Cooked Stadium Beans

Diana Krol
Nickerson, KS

*I first tasted these beans at a friend's wedding rehearsal dinner.
I've been serving them ever since! It's my most-requested recipe,
wonderful for covered-dish dinners, picnics and of course tailgating.*

1/2 lb. bacon
1 onion, chopped
1 to 2 hot peppers, chopped
2 16-oz. cans baked beans,
   drained
16-oz. can kidney beans,
   drained
15-1/2 oz. can chili beans,
   drained

15-oz. can butter beans, drained
2 14-1/2 oz. cans green beans,
   drained
2/3 c. catsup
1/3 c. brown sugar, packed
1 t. chili powder
1/2 t. ground cumin

In a skillet over medium heat, cook bacon until crisp. Drain bacon on
paper towels, reserving drippings in skillet. Add onion and peppers to
drippings; sauté until tender. Combine all the beans in a slow cooker;
add crumbled bacon, onion mixture and any remaining drippings. In
a bowl, stir together catsup, brown sugar and spices; gently fold into
bean mixture. Cover and cook on low setting for 3 to 6 hours. May
also be placed in a greased 3 to 4-quart casserole dish and baked,
covered, at 350 degrees for one hour. Serves 12 to 16.

Pack a tailgating kit for the trunk. Fill a tote bag with paper
towels, wet wipes, trash bags, a bottle opener and matches for
the grill...all those must-haves that are so easy to forget. Now
enjoy your game day knowing that you're ready for anything!

Sweet Potato Cheese Ball

Tina George
El Dorado, AR

My family loves sweet potatoes! I usually prepare this scrumptious recipe the night before, so it's ready when we want it the next day. I like to use a mix of our favorite hot sauces.

8-oz. pkg. cream cheese, softened
2 c. cold mashed sweet potatoes
1/4 c. onion, finely chopped
2 T. jalapeño pepper, finely chopped
1 t. Worcestershire sauce

1-1/2 to 2 t. hot pepper sauce, or to taste
1 t. seasoned salt
1/4 c. chopped pecans
crackers, bread sticks or vegetable slices

In a large bowl, beat cream cheese and sweet potatoes until smooth. Add remaining ingredients except crackers, bread sticks or vegetable slices; mix well. Cover and refrigerate for 4 hours, or until easy to handle. Form into a ball; wrap well and refrigerate for an additional 4 hours, until firm. Serve with crackers, bread sticks or vegetables. Makes about 3 cups.

Be sure to have some finger foods for the kids...tortilla pinwheels, cheese cubes, apple wedges and mini pigs-in-a-blanket are terrific for little tailgaters.

Kicky Cheese Spread

Sharri Cadigan
Hagerstown, MD

When I made this cheese spread for a Halloween party, it got rave reviews. It has an afterbite...it's so good, it's almost scary!

8-oz. pkg. cream cheese,
   softened
8-oz. container spreadable
   cream cheese with chive &
   onion
2 c. shredded sharp Cheddar
   cheese
1 c. shredded 4-cheese Mexican
   blend

1 T. Worcestershire sauce
1/4 t. cayenne pepper, or more
   to taste
1 t. paprika
5 to 6 slices bacon, crisply
   cooked and crumbled
tortilla chips, crackers and
   vegetable slices

In a large bowl, blend cream cheeses. Add shredded cheeses, Worcestershire sauce, pepper and paprika. Stir in bacon. Cover and chill for at least 4 hours. Transfer to a serving container, or form into a ball or log. Serve with tortilla chips, crackers and vegetable slices. Makes about 18 servings.

Create quick chip & dip sets in no time. Spoon dips into pottery soup bowls and set each bowl on a dinner plate. Surround with crackers, veggies, pretzels, chips or bread for dipping.

Football Party Pizza Dip

Gladys Kielar
Perrysburg, OH

This appetizer is terrific for family football parties. We love it.

8-oz. pkg. cream cheese,
   softened
3/4 c. pizza sauce
1 t. Italian seasoning
2 T. red pepper, chopped

2 T. green pepper, chopped
1/2 c. grated Parmesan cheese
1/2 c. shredded mozzarella
   cheese
crackers, vegetable slices

Spread cream cheese in a microwave-safe 9" pie plate; top with pizza sauce. Sprinkle with remaining ingredients except crackers and vegetable slices in order given. Microwave, uncovered, on high for 2 minutes, or until heated through. Serve warm with crackers and vegetable slices. Makes 8 to 10 servings.

Cool-weather fun makes everyone hungry, so take along some treats for munching. Pick up some new paper paint pails from the hardware store to decorate with cut-outs and paint. Fill with snack mix or popcorn and wrap up in clear cellophane...yum!

Holiday Herb Dip

Paula Marchesi
Lenhartsville, PA

This delicious, easy-to-make dip is our family's favorite. Just watch your guests' eyes light up when they taste it! I like to double this recipe, then serve one bowl surrounded with veggies and the other with chips and pretzels.

3/4 c. mayonnaise
3/4 c. sour cream
1 t. green onion, minced
1 t. fresh chives, minced
1 t. capers, drained
1/2 t. salt
1/2 t. lemon juice

1/2 t. Worcestershire sauce
1/4 t. fresh parsley, minced
1/4 t. paprika
1/4 t. curry powder
1/8 t. garlic salt
assorted vegetable slices, chips
   and pretzels

In a serving bowl, combine all ingredients except vegetables, chips and pretzels. Blend well. Cover and refrigerate for one hour. Serve with vegetable slices, chips and pretzels. Makes 1-1/2 cups.

A person who can bring the spirit of laughter
into a room is indeed blessed.

–Bennett Cerf

Game-Day Subs

Tammy Farren
Omaha, NE

*A super-easy meal for watching sports on TV at home
or toting along in a picnic cooler.*

1/4 lb. hard salami, chopped
1/4 lb. deli ham, chopped
1/4 lb. pepperoni, chopped
1/4 lb. deli roast turkey,
    chopped
1 red onion, chopped

1 head lettuce, shredded
2 c. cherry tomatoes, halved
8-oz. pkg. shredded Swiss
    cheese
4 to 6 hoagie buns, split

In a large bowl, mix together all ingredients except buns. Spoon into hoagie buns. Drizzle with desired amount of Sub Dressing. Makes 4 to 6 servings.

Sub Dressing:

3/4 c. oil
1/4 c. tarragon vinegar
1/4 t. dried oregano

1/8 t. garlic powder
1 t. salt
1/8 t. pepper

Mix all ingredients together in a small bowl or a jar with a lid. Whisk or shake until blended.

A fireside cookout before a hometown football game is a
terrific idea on a brisk autumn night. Join the kids for
a friendly game of touch football, roast hot dogs, make
s'mores and tell ghost stories...what fun!

Festive Fall Flavors

Touchdown Pickle Dip

Angela Olson
Onamia, MN

You'll love this tasty twist on pickle roll-ups!

2 8-oz. pkgs. cream cheese
   softened
1 lb. deli shaved ham, finely
   chopped

32-oz. jar baby dill pickles,
   drained and juice reserved
round buttery crackers or
   cracker sticks

In a large bowl, blend cream cheese and ham. Finely chop pickles and stir in. Add 1/4 to 1/2 cup of reserved pickle juice; blend well. If dip seems too thick, add more pickle juice. Cover and chill until serving time. Serve with crackers or cracker sticks. Makes 12 to 18 servings.

Braunschweiger Spread

Amy Wrightsel
Louisville, KY

My mom and aunt have been making this tasty spread for over 35 years. Finally I wrote down the recipe as my mom prepared it. Now the family treasure is ready for sharing!

8-oz. pkg. braunschweiger,
   softened
8-oz. pkg. cream cheese,
   softened
1/3 c. mayonnaise

3 T. green olives, chopped
1 T. onion, chopped
1/4 t. garlic salt
hearty wheat crackers

Combine all ingredients except crackers in a large bowl; mix until well blended. Cover and chill until serving time. Serve with wheat crackers. Serves 8.

Paper coffee filters are great for serving up hoagies, tacos, wraps and burgers...no spills, no mess and easy to hold!

Hot Wing Dip

Bobbie Termeer
Powell, OH

This irresistible slow-cooker dip tastes just like everyone's favorite hot buffalo wings...it's a party in a crock!

20-oz. can chicken breast,
   drained and flaked
3/4 c. hot pepper sauce
2 8-oz. pkgs. cream cheese,
   softened

1 c. ranch salad dressing
8-oz. pkg. shredded Cheddar or
   Colby cheese, divided
chips or crackers, celery sticks

Combine chicken and hot sauce in a skillet over medium heat; cook until heated through. Stir in cream cheese and salad dressing. Cook and stir until warm and well blended. Mix in 3/4 cup shredded cheese; transfer mixture to a slow cooker. Sprinkle remaining cheese on top. Cover and cook on low setting for 3 to 4 hours, until hot and bubbly. Serve with chips or crackers and celery sticks. Makes 15 to 20 servings.

Serve your favorite yummy hot or cold dip spooned into crisp wonton cups...so easy, yet so impressive on an appetizer tray! Coat a muffin tin with non-stick vegetable spray, then press a wonton wrapper gently into each cup. Spritz with a little more of the spray and bake at 350 degrees for 8 minutes, or until golden. Fill as desired.

Festive Fall Flavors

Hot & Sticky Maple Wings
Donna Achenbach
Fort Wayne, IN

Be sure to have plenty of napkins handy...these wings are very gooey, but tasty! They can be prepped in advance and marinated in the refrigerator for 24 hours before baking.

1/2 c. maple syrup
1/4 c. hot pepper sauce
1/4 c. soy sauce
2 cloves garlic, minced

1/4 t. red pepper flakes
2 lbs. chicken wings
Garnish: blue cheese or ranch
    salad dressing, celery sticks

In a large bowl, combine maple syrup, sauces and garlic. Reserve 1/3 cup of syrup mixture; add wings to remaining sauce in bowl. Toss to coat; cover and refrigerate 3 hours. Refrigerate reserved syrup mixture separately. Drain wings and discard marinade. Place wings in a shallow baking pan lined with aluminum foil. Bake at 400 degrees for 25 minutes, turning over after 15 minutes. Heat broiler. Broil wings for 5 minutes, or until golden and juices run clear. Toss wings with reserved syrup mixture. Serve with desired salad dressing and celery sticks on the side. Makes 6 to 8 servings.

G-hosting a Halloween buffet? Offer a selection of creepy foods and beverages, labeled with table tents in your spookiest handwriting. Have a specialty that isn't Halloween-inspired? Just give it a spooky new name!

Brisket Roll Sandwiches
Kimberley O'Rourke
Irving, TX

A genuine southern treat! So easy to prepare with a slow cooker.

3-lb. boneless beef brisket
1/2 c. Dijon mustard
1/2 c. yellow mustard

1-1/2 oz. pkg. onion soup mix
8 potato rolls, split

Place brisket in a large slow cooker; set aside. Mix mustards together in a small bowl; brush over brisket. Sprinkle with soup mix. Cover and cook on low setting for 7 to 8 hours, until very tender. Allow brisket to cool slightly; slice thinly and serve on rolls. Serves 8.

Make a stack of comfy sit-upons for sports nights and picnicking. Cut a 30-inch by 15-inch rectangle of colorful vinyl...a dollar-store tablecloth is perfect. Fold in half and punch holes around the 3 cut sides. Stitch two sides with yarn and a big needle, tuck in a foam square to make it nice and comfy, then stitch the last side and slip-stitch the opening closed.

Festive Fall Flavors

Confetti Corn & Bean Dip

Karen Schmidt
Racine, WI

A friend shared this old recipe with me years ago and I've since added a new twist or two to punch up the flavor.

15-1/4 oz. can corn, drained
16-oz. can black beans, drained
   and rinsed
1 red onion, diced
4 roma tomatoes, diced
2 jalapeño peppers, diced

juice of 2 limes
1/2 bunch fresh cilantro,
   snipped
2 avocados, halved, pitted and
   diced
salt to taste

In a large bowl, mix together all ingredients. Cover and chill. Makes about 12 servings.

Fill a punch bowl with assorted half-masks, funny glasses, mini hats and other disguises for party guests to choose from...just for fun!

Bacon-Cheddar Cups

Susan Gudzinowicz
Litchfield, NH

We can't keep enough of these easy, delicious bite-size appetizers on hand! I always have four to five batches tucked in our freezer, ready for the next invitation to a football celebration or dinner party.

2 c. shredded sharp Cheddar
   cheese
1 c. mayonnaise
3.8-oz. can sliced black olives,
   drained

4-oz. pkg. bacon bits
2 T. onion, chopped
2 to 3 2.1-oz. pkgs. frozen
   mini phyllo shells

Combine all ingredients except phyllo shells in a bowl; mix thoroughly. Add a heaping tablespoon of cheese mixture to each phyllo shell. Place shells on an ungreased baking sheet. Bake at 300 degrees for 15 to 20 minutes, until cheese mixture is melted. For a freeze-ahead appetizer, fill shells, place on a tray, wrap and freeze...no need to thaw before baking. Makes 30 to 45.

Mix up Frankie's Nuts & Bolts Mix in a jiffy...it's frightfully good!
Just toss together 2 cups pretzel sticks, 2 cups ring-shaped pretzels,
one cup mixed nuts and 1/2 cup golden raisins.

Cheesy Spinach-Artichoke Dip *Judy Scherer*
Benton, MO

A slow-cooker recipe that's great for a party and really simple to make.

2 8-oz. pkgs. cream cheese, softened
3/4 c. half-and-half
10-oz. pkg. frozen chopped spinach, thawed and drained
13-oz. can artichoke hearts, drained and chopped
1 T. onion, finely chopped

1 clove garlic, minced
2/3 c. shredded Monterey Jack cheese
1/2 c. shredded Parmesan cheese
tortilla chips or thin wheat crackers

In a large bowl, combine cream cheese and half-and-half; mix until well blended. Add spinach, artichokes, onion and garlic; stir well. Transfer mixture to a slow cooker. Cover and cook on high setting for 1-1/2 to 2 hours, until warmed through. At serving time, sprinkle with shredded cheeses. Serve with chips or crackers. Makes 8 servings.

Turn mini Jack-Be-Little pumpkins into real characters!
Just add candy wax lips or plastic teeth and thumbtack eyes.
Heaped in a bowl, they make fun take-home favors.

Harvest Cider

Vickie

This spiced beverage will warm you up after football cheering, trick-or-treating or just a brisk walk around the neighborhood to savor the colorful autumn leaves.

12-oz. can frozen apple juice concentrate
12-oz. can frozen cranberry-apple juice concentrate
6-oz. can frozen lemonade concentrate
9 c. water
5 4-inch cinnamon sticks
1 t. whole nutmeg, coarsely chopped
7 whole cloves
Optional: 1/3 c. cinnamon schnapps
Garnish: additional cinnamon sticks

In a stockpot over medium-low heat, combine frozen concentrates and water. Stir well as juices melt. Add spices, enclosed in a muslin spice bag. Bring to a boil. Reduce heat to low; cover and simmer for 15 minutes. Discard spice bag; stir in schnapps, if using. Pour into mugs; garnish with cinnamon sticks for stirring. Serves 12.

French Iced Coffee

Ruby Pruitt
Nashville, IN

We girls started going over to Mom's for breakfast every couple weeks after my dad passed away. I thought my siblings would enjoy something different, so I brought this coffee. Even my choosiest sister loved it! This is a terrific make-ahead recipe too.

2 c. sugar
3 c. strong brewed regular or decaf coffee
4 c. regular or fat-free milk
2 c. regular or fat-free whipping cream
2 t. vanilla extract

In a large pitcher, dissolve sugar in hot coffee; cool. Add remaining ingredients. Pour into one to 2 freezer-safe containers; cover and freeze 8 hours to overnight. To serve, let stand at room temperature for 2 hours; chop up with a spoon. Serves 10.

Festive Fall
Flavors

Touchdown Doughnut Balls

Cindy Long
Xenia, OH

*There's nothing more delicious than a homemade doughnut!
These bite-size morsels are delicious with cider.*

3 c. pancake mix
1/3 c. sugar
1-1/2 t. cinnamon
1/2 t. nutmeg
2 eggs, beaten

3/4 c. milk
2 T. oil, plus oil for deep frying
Garnish: powdered sugar or
    cinnamon-sugar

In a large bowl, combine pancake mix, sugar, spices, eggs, milk and 2 tablespoons oil. Stir until well mixed; set aside. Place several inches of oil in a deep saucepan; heat to 375 degrees over medium-high heat. Drop batter by teaspoonfuls into hot oil, a few at a time. Cook, turning frequently, until golden on all sides. Doughnuts will cook quickly, so watch carefully. Drain on paper towels. When cooled slightly, dust doughnuts with powdered sugar or cinnamon-sugar. Serves 6 to 8.

Host a neighborhood spruce-up! Everyone can help rake leaves, trim bushes, pull bloomed-out annuals...kids can help too. Afterwards, share cider and doughnuts for a perfect ending to a fun get-together.

Halloween Popcorn Balls

Scarlett Thornley
Port St. John, FL

Our family has made these yummy popcorn balls for years. The recipe makes plenty for family and little trick-or-treaters to share!

12 c. popped popcorn
1 c. candy corn
1/4 c. margarine

10-1/2 oz. pkg. mini
marshmallows
3-oz. pkg. orange gelatin mix

Place popcorn and candy corn in a large heat-proof bowl; toss to mix and set aside. Combine margarine and marshmallows in a microwave-safe dish. Microwave on high for about 2 minutes, until melted. Add dry gelatin mix and stir well. Pour marshmallow mixture over popcorn mixture; stir to coat well. With greased or moistened hands, form into 15 balls. Wrap popcorn balls in plastic wrap or small Halloween treat bags; tie with ribbon or raffia. Makes 15.

Popcorn ball funny faces! Set out a variety of small candies like gumdrops, candy corn, candy-coated chocolates and licorice whips. Kids can have fun using dabs of marshmallow creme or frosting to make their own creations.

Save Room for Dessert

enjoy!

Upside-Down Apple-Pecan Pie

Francine Bryson
Pickens, SC

When I was a child, both my grandmas used to make this pie. Nana gave Granny the recipe and they took turns making it for holidays. Over the years, I tweaked it and even won the North Carolina State Apple Cook-Off Grand Champion with it. You can use any mix of sweet and tart cooking apples.

1/2 c. butter, softened
1-1/2 c. pecan halves
1-1/2 c. brown sugar, packed
2 9-inch pie crusts
1/2 c. sugar
2 T. lemon juice
1 t. vanilla extract
3 T. all-purpose flour

1 T. apple pie spice
1-1/8 t. cinnamon
1/2 t. nutmeg
3 c. Honey Crisp apples, peeled, cored and sliced
3 c. Swiss Gourmet apples, peeled, cored and sliced
Garnish: vanilla ice cream

Spread softened butter in the bottom and up the sides of a 9" deep-dish pie plate. Arrange pecan halves over butter, flat-side up, to cover pie plate. Sprinkle brown sugar over pecans. Place one pie crust on top of brown sugar; press into pie plate and set aside. In a large bowl, combine sugar, lemon juice, vanilla, flour and spices; mix well. Add apples and toss until coated. Spoon apple mixture evenly into pie crust. Cover with remaining pie crust; fold over edges and crimp together. (This will be the bottom of the pie, so don't worry about how it looks.) Pierce crust several times with a fork. Bake at 450 degrees for 10 minutes; reduce heat to 350 degrees and bake for another 45 minutes. Remove from oven; let stand briefly until the bubbling stops. While pie is still hot, invert a serving plate over pie and flip pie over onto plate. Pecans will now be on top. Serve warm, topped with scoops of ice cream. Makes 8 servings.

Host a neighborhood pie party! Invite everyone to tie on an apron and bring their best-loved pie to share, along with extra copies of the recipe. Bring home some new-to-you recipes...one of them just might become a favorite!

Gingersnap Pumpkin Pie

*Sarah Phillip
Tuckerton, NJ*

A delicious combination! I tried this recipe for Thanksgiving because I am not a big fan of ordinary pie crust...it was a huge hit with my family.

15-oz. can pumpkin
14-oz. can sweetened condensed
  milk
2 eggs, beaten

2 T. pumpkin pie spice
1/8 t. salt
Garnish: additional pumpkin
  pie spice

In a bowl, blend pumpkin and condensed milk. Add eggs, spice and salt; mix well. Pour into Gingersnap Crust; sprinkle with additional spice. Bake at 425 degrees for 15 minutes; reduce oven to 350 degrees and bake for another 35 minutes, or until set. Makes 8 servings.

Gingersnap Crust:

1-1/2 c. to 2 c. gingersnap
  cookies, crushed
Optional: 2 T. hazelnuts,
  crushed

3/4 to 1 c. butter, melted

In a bowl, toss crushed cookies and nuts, if using, with melted butter. Press mixture into a 9" pie plate, making a 1/4-inch thick crust in the bottom and up the sides of pie plate.

Take a harvest-time family outing to a farm. Many are open to the public for good old-fashioned fun like pumpkin picking, corn mazes and hayrides. You'll enjoy it as much as the kids!

Halloween Poke Cake

Eleanor Dionne
Beverly, MA

*Young and old alike love this easy recipe...it's become
a Halloween tradition at my house.*

18-1/4 oz. pkg. fudge marble
    cake mix
6-oz. pkg. orange gelatin mix
1 c. boiling water
1/2 c. cold water
1/2 c. butter, softened

3-1/2 c. powdered sugar
1/3 c. baking cocoa
1/4 c. milk
1 t. vanilla extract
Garnish: candy pumpkins or
    candy corn

Prepare and bake cake mix according to package directions, using
a greased 13"x9" baking pan. Cool cake in pan on a wire rack for
one hour. In a bowl, dissolve gelatin mix in boiling water; stir in cold
water. With a large fork or a wooden skewer, poke holes in cake, about
2 inches apart. Slowly pour gelatin over cake. Cover and refrigerate for
2 hours. In a large bowl, beat butter until fluffy. Beat in powdered
sugar, cocoa, milk and vanilla until smooth. Spread over cake; top
with candies. Keep chilled until serving time. Serves 10 to 12.

S'mores cupcakes in a jiffy! Bake your favorite chocolate cupcakes,
but remove them from the oven with 3 minutes baking time left.
Top each cupcake with a marshmallow. Return to the oven
and finish baking for 3 minutes, or until the marshmallows
are toasty and golden. Sprinkle crushed graham crackers
over the marshmallows, if you like.

Caramel Apple Cake

Liz Davies
Spanish Fork, UT

*This scrumptious dessert is a family favorite
all year 'round. It's oh-so easy to make too.*

18-1/2 oz. pkg. yellow cake mix
21-oz. can apple pie filling
2 eggs, beaten

12-oz. jar caramel ice cream
topping, divided
Garnish: vanilla ice cream

Grease and flour a 13"x9" baking pan and set aside. In a bowl, combine dry cake mix, pie filling, eggs and 1/4 cup caramel topping. Beat with an electric beater on low speed for one to 2 minutes, until blended. Pour batter into baking pan. Bake at 350 degrees for 30 to 35 minutes. Remove cake from oven. Pour remaining caramel topping over cake and spread evenly. Serve topped with ice cream. Serves 8 to 10.

When I was little, there was no greater thrill for me than staying with my Mamaw & Papaw Brickey on their mountain farm. I enjoyed exploring the farm's old barn and smokehouse as well as the woods nearby. Papaw would let my younger cousin Lynn, who lived close by, and me go out into the cornfield and knock down dried cornstalks, which we thought was great fun! In the evenings we would be treated to bedtime stories by Mamaw, who was the best storyteller ever. Her spooky tales could make the hair stand up on your head! If I was lucky, she took me trick-or-treating to the closest neighbors' houses. It was a yummy change for me...homemade caramel apples and popcorn balls instead of store-bought candy! I am so blessed that I have my wonderful Mamaw still with me. She's in her nineties now, but her memory is just as clear as ever. We thoroughly enjoy reminiscing and laughing over those good ol' days!

–Carol Hickman, Kingsport, TN

Signature Chocolate Cream Pie

Kay Little
Diana, TX

This is an easy, tried & true recipe that I have passed down to my daughter, Jennifer. It is just what you want in a chocolate pie...a rich, intense chocolate filling dressed up with whipped cream. And the filling takes only a few minutes to make!

3 egg yolks	3 T. baking cocoa
1-1/2 c. whole milk	1/4 t. salt
1 c. sugar	2 T. butter
2 T. all-purpose flour	1 t. vanilla extract
2 T. cornstarch	9-inch pie crust, baked

In a large bowl, beat egg yolks and milk with an electric mixer on low speed until blended. In a separate bowl, mix sugar, flour, cornstarch, cocoa and salt. Add to egg mixture; blend well. Pour mixture into a microwave-safe bowl. Microwave on high setting for 6 to 8 minutes, until thickened, stirring well at 2-minute intervals. Add butter and vanilla; stir well. Immediately pour mixture into baked pie crust. Cool to room temperature; cover and refrigerate for one hour. Serve topped with dollops of Sweetened Whipped Cream. Serves 6 to 8.

Sweetened Whipped Cream:

2 c. whipping cream, chilled	1 t. vanilla extract
1/2 c. powdered sugar	

With an electric mixer on medium-high speed, whip cream until soft peaks form. Add powdered sugar and vanilla; whip until stiff peaks form.

Rose's Black Midnight Cake

Karen Boehme
Greensburg, PA

My mom's signature dessert, this recipe has been in our family all my life. It's the cake we enjoyed for birthdays, picnics and other family gatherings. As either a layer cake or a sheet cake, it is divine.

2/3 c. shortening
1-2/3 c. sugar
3 eggs
2/3 c. baking cocoa
1-1/3 c. cold water
2-1/4 c. all-purpose flour

1/3 t. baking powder
1-1/4 t. baking soda
1 t. salt
1 t. vanilla extract
Garnish: powdered sugar or
    fudge frosting

Grease a 13"x9" baking pan or two 9" round cake pans; set aside. In a large bowl, blend shortening and sugar until fluffy. Beat in eggs, one at a time; set aside. In a small bowl, stir together cocoa and water. In a separate bowl, mix flour, baking powder, baking soda and salt. Add flour mixture to shortening mixture alternately with cocoa mixture; stir in vanilla. Pour batter into pans. Bake at 350 degrees until a toothpick inserted in center tests clean, 35 to 45 minutes for a 13"x9" pan or 30 to 35 minutes for two 9" pans. Cool; garnish as desired. Serves 12 to 16.

The haunts of happiness are varied,
but I have more often found her among little children,
home firesides and country houses than anywhere else.

–Sydney Smith

Grandma's Cherry Pudding Cake

Linda Basham
Morris, IL

Grandma made this cake with fresh cherries from our trees every summer. I still enjoy picking the cherries to make this dessert.

1/4 c. butter, softened
2 c. sugar, divided
2 c. all-purpose flour
4 t. baking powder

1 c. milk
1 c. hot water
2 c. sour cherries, pitted
Garnish: vanilla ice cream

In a bowl, blend butter and one cup sugar; set aside. In a separate bowl, mix flour and baking powder. Add flour mixture and milk alternately to butter mixture. Stir until smooth; turn into a buttered 8"x8" baking pan. In another bowl, mix remaining sugar, hot water and cherries. Pour over batter in pan; do not stir. Bake, uncovered, at 350 degrees for 40 minutes. Carefully remove pan from oven. Dessert will be thin on the bottom, with cherries and cake on top. As it cools, the bottom layer will thicken into a sauce. Serve warm, scooping out cake and spooning some sauce over top. Garnish with a scoop of ice cream. Serves 9.

Brown Sugar Nut Pie

Linda Belon
Wintersville, OH

I love to try this recipe with a mix of nuts from the farmers' market...pecans, walnuts, hickory nuts. Yummy!

1 c. brown sugar, packed
1/2 c. sugar
1 egg, beaten
1 T. milk

9-inch pie crust
1/2 to 1 c. halved or chopped
   nuts
Garnish: whipped cream

In a bowl, stir together sugars, egg and milk. Pour into unbaked pie crust; arrange nuts on top. Bake at 325 degrees for 50 to 55 minutes, until completely set in the middle. Cool completely before cutting. Top with dollops of whipped cream. Makes 6 to 8 servings.

Country Harvest Pie

Janis Parr
Ontario, Canada

*This pie looks and tastes amazing. The cranberries give it color
and complement the sweet mellowness of the apples
and pears. Everyone loves it!*

2 9-inch pie crusts
3 McIntosh apples, peeled, cored
   and thickly sliced
3 Bartlett pears, peeled, cored
   and sliced
3/4 c. fresh cranberries
3/4 c. sugar

3 T. all-purpose flour
1/4 t. cinnamon
1 T. milk
2 t. butter, sliced
Optional: whipped cream or
   vanilla ice cream

Place one pie crust in a 9" pie plate; set aside. In a large bowl, combine
apples, pears, cranberries and sugar; set aside. In a small bowl, mix
together flour and cinnamon; combine with fruit mixture. Sprinkle milk
over fruit mixture; stir well. Spoon into pie crust; dot with butter. Add
top crust; crimp edges and cut several vents. Bake at 425 degrees for
15 minutes. Reduce oven to 350 degrees and continue baking for
35 to 45 minutes, until apples are tender. Garnish with whipped
cream or ice cream, if desired. Serves 6 to 8.

Mini tarts are just right after a hearty Thanksgiving dinner.
With a 4-inch biscuit cutter, cut 6 circles from a pie crust. Press
gently into ungreased muffin cups. Spoon 2 tablespoons apple
or cherry pie filling into each cup. Bake at 425 degrees for
14 to 18 minutes, until bubbly and golden. So sweet!

Buttermilk Pear Cobbler

Trysha Mapley
Palmer, AK

This recipe was inspired by my Grandmother Doris. She likely made a similar dessert on the farm in upstate New York when she was raising her children. It is a country cobbler topped with a lightly sweetened, soft buttermilk biscuit. Absolute comfort food!

3 lbs. Anjou or Bosc pears,
   peeled, cored and sliced
1/3 c. brown sugar, packed
1 T. all-purpose flour

1 T. lemon juice
1 t. cinnamon
1/4 t. nutmeg
1/4 t. mace

Combine all ingredients in a large bowl; toss gently to coat pears. Spoon pear mixture into an 8"x8" baking pan coated with non-stick vegetable spray. Drop Biscuit Topping by heaping tablespoonfuls onto pear mixture. Bake at 350 degrees for 45 minutes, or until lightly golden and bubbly. Makes 8 servings.

Biscuit Topping:

1 c. all-purpose flour
1 T. baking powder
3 T. buttermilk

2 T. sugar
1/2 c. chilled butter
3/4 c. milk

In a bowl, mix together flour, baking powder, buttermilk and sugar. Cut in butter with a fork until mixture is crumbly; add milk and mix well.

Finding out at the last minute you're in charge of treats for the after-school get-together? Just fill a market basket with fresh fruit and fruit dip for a yummy and healthy treat.

Cheddar Crumble Apple Pie JoAnn

Warm apple pie is delicious topped with a slice of Cheddar cheese.
This clever recipe bakes the Cheddar right into the pie. Give it a try!

1/2 c. sugar
1/2 c. brown sugar, packed
3/4 t. cinnamon
11-oz. pkg. pie crust mix,
   divided
3 T. chilled butter
2 c. shredded sharp Cheddar
   cheese, divided

2 to 2-1/2 T. water
3 lbs. tart apples, peeled, cored
   and sliced
1 T. all-purpose flour
sugar and nutmeg to taste
Optional: vanilla ice cream

In a large bowl, combine sugars, cinnamon and half of dry pie crust mix. Cut in butter with a fork until crumbly; set aside. In a separate bowl, combine remaining pie crust mix and one cup cheese. Stir in water until dough forms. Roll out dough on a floured surface; line a 9" pie plate. In a separate bowl, toss apples with flour; add sugar and nutmeg to taste. Spoon apples into pie crust; top with half of sugar mixture, remaining cheese and remaining sugar mixture. Bake at 375 degrees for about 40 minutes, or until topping is golden and apples are tender. Serve warm, topped with ice cream if desired. Makes 6 to 8 servings.

A fun way to serve cake pops or lollipops! Simply drill holes
in the top of a pumpkin and insert the treat sticks.

Walnut Frosties

Michele Maust
Rawlings, MD

These cookies are fabulous and always a pleaser for anyone who loves nuts and rich flavors! The recipe came to me via my husband's Mennonite background. They freeze well.

2 c. all-purpose flour
1/2 t. baking soda
1/4 t. salt
1/2 c. butter, softened

1 c. brown sugar, packed
1 egg, beaten
1 t. vanilla extract

In a bowl, combine flour, baking soda and salt; set aside. In a separate large bowl, blend butter and brown sugar together. Add egg and vanilla; beat well. Gradually add flour mixture to butter mixture; stir well. Cover and refrigerate for one to 2 hours. Roll dough into one-inch balls; arrange on lightly greased baking sheets. Make a thumbprint in the center of each cookie; fill each thumbprint with one teaspoon Nut Topping. Bake at 350 degrees for 8 to 10 minutes, until cookies are slightly soft to the touch; do not overbake. Cool on wire racks; store in an airtight container between layers of wax paper. Makes 4 to 5 dozen.

Nut Topping:

1 c. walnuts, finely chopped
1/2 c. brown sugar, packed

1/4 c. sour cream

Stir all ingredients together.

A simple harvest decoration for cupcakes! Cut red, yellow and orange fruit-flavored snack rolls with leaf-shaped mini cookie cutters, then press the "leaves" onto frosted cupcakes.

Save Room for Dessert

Autumn Pumpkin Bars

Jessica Jacoby
Temecula, CA

Every year on September 1st, I make a batch of these bars.
I continue to make them through the holidays. They have been
a family favorite for years. Easy and delicious!

2 c. canned pumpkin	1 t. baking soda
1 c. oil or applesauce	1 t. salt
4 eggs, beaten	2 t. cinnamon
1 t. vanilla extract	1 t. ground ginger
2 c. sugar	1/2 t. ground cloves
2 c. all-purpose flour	

In a large bowl, whisk together pumpkin, oil or applesauce, eggs and vanilla; set aside. In a separate bowl, combine remaining ingredients; mix well and stir into pumpkin mixture. Spread in an ungreased 13"x9" baking pan. Bake at 350 degrees for 20 to 25 minutes. Cool; cut into bars. Makes 3 dozen.

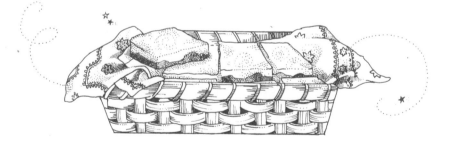

Clean-up is a snap for bar cookies...just line the baking pan
with aluminum foil before adding the dough, leaving a foil
"handle" extending on each side. Once the cookies have
completely cooled, lift out the cookies by the handles,
peel off the foil and cut into bars.

Chocolate-Bacon Cupcakes

Brenda Lautenschlaeger
Grand Haven, MI

My bacon-loving husband suggested I try this
unusual recipe...we agreed it is delicious!

2 c. all-purpose flour
3/4 c. plus 1 T. baking cocoa,
   divided
2 c. sugar
1 t. baking powder
2 t. baking soda
1/2 t. salt

2 eggs, beaten
1 c. strong brewed coffee, cooled
1 c. buttermilk
1/2 c. oil
12 slices bacon, crisply cooked,
   crumbled and divided
Garnish: chocolate frosting

In a large bowl, stir together flour, 3/4 cup baking cocoa, sugar,
baking powder, baking soda and salt. Make a well in the center; add
eggs, coffee, buttermilk and oil. Stir just until blended; mix in 3/4 of
bacon. Spoon batter into greased or paper-lined muffin cups, filling
2/3 full. Bake at 375 degrees for 20 to 25 minutes, until tops spring
back when lightly pressed. Set muffin tin on a wire rack to cool. Frost
cupcakes; sprinkle with remaining bacon and dust with remaining
cocoa. Makes 2 dozen.

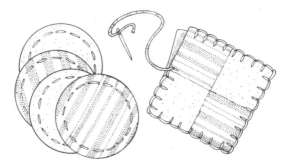

Turn an old wool sweater into some cozy mug coasters...
it's easy! Felt the sweater by setting the washing machine to
a hot wash and a cold rinse, then machine-dry on hot.
Cut out circles or squares. Decorate the edge with colorful
yarn in a simple whip stitch.

Jumbo Candy Cookies

Lisa Sett
Thousand Oaks, CA

*A bake-sale favorite that's a terrific way to use up
all that extra Halloween candy!*

18-1/2 oz. pkg. devil's food
   cake mix
1/2 c. oil

2 eggs, lightly beaten
6 fun-size chocolate bars, any
   variety, cut into large chunks

In a large bowl, mix dry cake mix and remaining ingredients; stir together. Form dough into golf ball-size balls. Place on parchment paper-lined baking sheets, about 3-1/2 inches apart. Bake at 350 degrees for 10 to 15 minutes. Cool before removing from baking sheets. Makes 2 dozen.

Back when pumpkin patches were more like farms than amusement parks, my family would pack up the van with our picnic dinner and head out to get pumpkins. We always took the same picnic foods...boiled hot dogs kept warm in a thermos, the same potato chips and the same cookies year-in and year-out.

Years & years later we still refer to that kind of cookie as "Pumpkin Patch" cookies. The five of us would enjoy our cozy picnic and head out to the patch to look for our pumpkins. My brother Chad would want the biggest possible pumpkin, my sister Heather wanted the "perfect" pumpkin and I always wanted the unusual pumpkin...green, or square, and once with quite a bit of the vine still attached. I can see it perfectly in my mind and will always cherish these family pumpkin patch memories.

–Heidi Walz, Omaha, NE

Frosted Pumpkin Cookies

Michel Johnson
Alexandria, MN

Topped with old-fashioned penuche frosting, these spiced cookies taste like a bite of autumn. Perfect for Halloween!

1/2 c. sugar
1/2 c. brown sugar, packed
1 c. butter, softened
1 c. canned pumpkin
1 egg, beaten
1 t. vanilla extract
2 c. all-purpose flour

1 t. baking powder
1 t. baking soda
1 t. cinnamon
1/4 t. salt
3/4 c. chopped walnuts or
    pecans

In a bowl, beat sugars and butter together until light and fluffy. Add pumpkin, egg and vanilla; blend well. Add remaining ingredients except nuts; mix well. Stir in nuts. Drop dough by rounded teaspoonfuls onto ungreased baking sheets, 2 inches apart. Bake at 350 degrees for 10 to 12 minutes, until edges are lightly golden. Immediately remove cookies to wire racks. Cool; spread with Penuche Frosting. Allow frosting to set before storing. Makes 5 dozen.

Penuche Frosting:

3 T. butter
1/2 c. brown sugar, packed

1/4 c. milk
1-1/2 to 2 c. powdered sugar

In a saucepan over medium heat, combine butter and brown sugar. Bring to a boil. Cook, stirring constantly, for one minute, or until slightly thickened. Allow to cool 10 minutes. Add milk and beat until smooth. Beat in powdered sugar to desired consistency.

When the temperature is dropping, treat yourself to a cup of warm mulled cider. Heat a mug of cider to boiling, add an orange spice teabag and let stand several minutes. Mmm!

Save Room for Dessert

Orange Gingerbread Cut-Outs
Zoe Bennett
Columbia, SC

Fresh orange zest gives these gingerbread cookies an extra zing!
One of my favorite cookie recipes from early fall until
the end of the holiday season.

2-3/4 c. all-purpose flour
1/2 t. baking soda
1/2 t. salt
1 t. ground ginger
2/3 c. light molasses
1/3 c. brown sugar, packed

1/3 c. butter, softened
1 egg, beaten
2 t. orange zest
Garnish: colored sugar,
mini candies

In a bowl, mix flour, baking soda, salt and ginger; set aside. In a separate large bowl, combine molasses, brown sugar, butter, egg and orange zest. Beat with an electric mixer on medium speed until smooth and creamy. Add flour mixture; beat on low speed until well mixed. Divide dough into 2 balls. Cover and refrigerate one to 2 hours, until firm. Using one ball of dough at a time, roll out 1/4-inch thick on a well-floured surface. Cut out with desired cookie cutters. Place on greased baking sheets, one inch apart. Bake at 375 degrees for 6 to 8 minutes, until cookies spring back when touched. Cool completely on wire racks. Decorate cookies as desired with Powdered Sugar Frosting, colored sugar and candies. Makes about 4 dozen.

Powdered Sugar Frosting:

4 c. powdered sugar
1/2 c. butter, softened
2 t. vanilla extract

3 to 4 T. milk
Optional: few drops food
coloring

Combine powdered sugar, butter and vanilla in a large bowl. Beat with an electric mixer on low speed, adding milk to desired consistency. Tint frosting with food coloring, if desired.

Make cookie giving fun...tuck a variety of wrapped cookies inside a pumpkin-shaped plastic pail. Remember to include copies of the recipes. All treats, no tricks!

Glazed Apple Cookies

Kelly Patrick
Ashburn, VA

This is a spin-off of my aunt's recipe for apple cake. These cookies filled with plump raisins are delicious in the fall. Mix them up by using different types of apples...sweet, tart or mild.

1 c. raisins
1-1/2 c. shortening
1-1/3 c. brown sugar, packed
1 egg, beaten
2 c. all-purpose flour
1 t. baking soda

1/2 t. salt
1/2 c. milk
1 c. chopped walnuts
1 c. apples, peeled, cored and
   finely chopped

Place raisins in a microwave-safe dish; add water to cover. Microwave on high for 4 to 5 minutes, until raisins are soft and plump. Drain well; set aside to cool. In a large bowl, blend together shortening, sugar and egg; set aside. In a separate bowl, blend flour, baking soda and salt. Add half of flour mixture to shortening mixture. Blend in milk and remaining flour mixture; fold in raisins, walnuts and apples. Drop by teaspoonfuls onto ungreased baking sheets, 2 inches apart. Bake at 400 degrees for 9 to 10 minutes. Drizzle warm cookies with Glaze. Makes 2 dozen.

Glaze:

1-1/2 c. powdered sugar
2-1/2 t. milk
1/4 t. vanilla extract

1 t. butter, melted
1/8 t. salt

Stir together all ingredients in a bowl.

Party fun! Fill a big jar with pieces of candy corn...don't forget to count them first. Ask everyone to guess how many pieces are in the jar...send the jar home with the person whose guess is the closest!

Save Room for Dessert

Cranberry-Orange Drops

Brenda Melancon
McComb, MS

This recipe is my favorite! The cookies are delectable and so easy to make since they start with boxed muffin mix.

1/3 c. butter, softened
2 7-oz. pkgs. cranberry muffin
   mix
1/3 c. brown sugar, packed
1 egg, beaten

1/2 t. orange extract
1/2 c. sweetened dried
   cranberries, chopped
1/2 c. chopped pecans, toasted

In a large bowl, combine butter, dry muffin mixes and brown sugar. Blend well; stir in egg and extract. Add cranberries and pecans; mix well. Drop by tablespoonfuls onto ungreased baking sheets, 2 inches apart. Bake at 350 degrees for 10 to 12 minutes, until golden around the edges. Cool on baking sheets for 2 minutes. Transfer to wire racks and cool completely. Makes 2-1/2 dozen.

Mix up some frosting for Halloween cookies...it's like magic! For orange pumpkins, add 6 drops yellow and 2 drops red food coloring to a small bowl of white frosting. For black bats, cats and witches' hats, add 2 to 3 drops blue food coloring to a small bowl of dark chocolate frosting.

Heavenly Key Lime Pie

Tina Goodpasture
Meadowview, VA

This refreshing pie is wonderful. It's simple to make, and its sweet-tart flavor is always welcome after a hearty meal.

14-oz. can sweetened
    condensed milk
3 egg yolks
2 t. Key lime zest
1/2 t. Key lime juice

9-inch graham cracker crust
1 c. whipping cream
2 T. powdered sugar
Optional: Key lime slices

In a bowl, whisk together condensed milk, egg yolks, lime zest and lime juice until well blended. Pour into pie crust. Bake at 350 degrees for about 15 minutes, until set. Cool completely, about one hour; cover and chill one hour before serving. Beat cream with an electric mixer on high speed for 2 to 3 minutes, until soft peaks form. Gradually beat in powdered sugar. Garnish pie with whipped cream and slices of lime, if desired. Serves 6 to 8.

Hot Lemon Pie

Sharon Ostrem
Ankeny, IA

Being retired and spending our winters in Tucson, Arizona, we find ourselves with an overabundance of lemons. My husband loves this pie and I love how easy it is to make!

1 large lemon, unpeeled, cut into
    chunks and seeds removed
1/2 c. sugar
4 eggs

1/2 c. margarine, sliced
1 t. vanilla extract
9-inch pie crust
Optional: whipped topping

Put all ingredients except crust and topping into a blender. Blend until mixture is foamy but smooth. Pour into unbaked crust. Bake at 350 degrees for 40 minutes, until filling sets up. Serve warm or chilled. Garnish with whipped topping, if desired. Serves 6 to 8.

Lemon Upside-Down Cake

Tiffany Brinkley
Broomfield, CO

My mother-in-law always brings us a box of fresh Meyer lemons when she comes from California for the holidays. This is one of my favorite ways to enjoy them!

3/4 c. butter, softened and
　divided
3/4 c. plus 2 T. brown sugar,
　packed
2 Meyer lemons, unpeeled,
　thinly sliced and seeds
　removed
1-1/2 c. all-purpose flour

2 t. baking powder
1/4 t. salt
1 c. sugar
1 t. vanilla extract
2 eggs, separated
3/4 c. milk
1/4 t. cream of tartar
Optional: whipped topping

Melt 1/4 cup butter in a 9" cast-iron skillet over medium heat. Stir in brown sugar until dissolved; remove from heat. Arrange lemon slices in skillet over brown sugar mixture; set aside. In a bowl, mix flour, baking powder and salt. In a separate large bowl, with an electric mixer on low speed, beat remaining butter and sugar until fluffy. Beat in vanilla and egg yolks, one at a time. Beat in flour mixture alternately with milk; set aside. In a separate bowl, with an electric mixer on high speed, beat egg whites and cream of tartar until stiff peaks form. Fold egg white mixture into batter. Spoon batter into skillet. Bake at 350 degrees for 30 minutes, or until a toothpick inserted in center tests clean. Let cake cool in skillet 15 minutes. Top skillet with a cake plate and turn cake out of skillet. Serve warm or at room temperature; garnish with whipped topping, if desired. Serves 8.

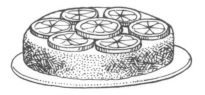

Add a scrumptious salty-sweet contrast to your favorite pie recipe with a pretzel crust. Mix 1-1/2 cups finely crushed pretzel crumbs, 1/4 cup sugar and 1/2 cup melted butter; press into a pie plate. Chill for 20 minutes or bake at 350 degrees for 10 minutes.

Vi's Fruit Cocktail Cake

Theresa Eldridge
Festus, MO

This is a simple and scrumptious cake. My mom (Mary Viola, or "Vi") always said that she "wasn't a fancy cook, just a good cook!" As a family member called out at a family reunion after tasting one of her delicious desserts, "Vi, you are looking at a mouthful of happiness here!" Although we lost her several years ago, the memories of her wonderful cooking live on.

2 c. all-purpose flour
1-1/2 c. sugar
2 t. baking soda
1/2 t. salt
2 eggs, beaten

15-1/4 oz. can fruit cocktail in
   heavy syrup
1 c. brown sugar, packed
3/4 c. chopped nuts

In a large bowl, stir together flour, sugar, baking soda and salt. Add eggs and undrained fruit cocktail; mix well. Spray a 13"x9" baking pan with non-stick butter-flavored vegetable spray; pour in batter. Mix brown sugar and nuts; sprinkle over batter. Bake at 350 degrees for 35 to 45 minutes, until cake tests done in the center with a toothpick. While cake is still hot, spoon Coconut Icing evenly over top; let cool. Icing will melt and make a delicious glaze over the cake. Makes 12 servings.

Coconut Icing:

1/2 c. sweetened flaked coconut
1/2 c. butter, softened

3/4 c. sugar

Stir ingredients together until well blended.

A tribute to Mom! A nostalgic tea towel makes a clever mat for framing your mother's most-treasured recipe. Include a picture of Mom in her kitchen...so sweet!

Save Room for Dessert

Raisin Squares

William Viveiros
Fall River, MA

This recipe has been in my wife's family for years, and I have been baking these squares for some time. If you like the rich flavor of raisins you will love this...oh, the taste!

2 c. orange juice
2 c. water
4 c. raisins
2 11-oz. pkgs. pie crust mix

1-1/3 c. sugar
1/2 c. all-purpose flour
5 T. lemon juice
1/8 t. salt

Combine orange juice and water in a large saucepan over medium heat. Bring to a boil. Remove from heat; stir in raisins. Let stand for 2 hours. Prepare pie crust mixes according to package directions; divide in half. Roll out half of pie crust on a floured surface; arrange crust in a 15"x10" jelly-roll pan and set aside. Return saucepan with raisin mixture to low heat. Add sugar, flour, lemon juice and salt. Cook, stirring constantly for about 10 minutes, until thickened. Spread raisin mixture into crust-lined pan. Roll out remaining pie crust; place over raisin mixture and seal edges. Bake at 350 degrees for about 30 to 40 minutes, until golden. Cool; cut into squares. Makes 4 dozen.

Make a sundae pie in a jiffy! Press a tube of refrigerated chocolate chip cookie dough into a 9" pie plate. Cover and chill for 30 minutes, then bake as package directs. Fill cooled cookie crust with scoops of ice cream, hot fudge topping, whipped cream and a maraschino cherry. Yummy!

Double Chocolate Tiramisu

Kim Wilson
Melbourne, FL

*I made this dessert for my daughter's birthday one year and
we were all hooked! It's definitely for chocolate lovers. Garnish
with chocolate shavings for an extra-special touch.*

2 T. baking cocoa
1-1/2 c. very hot water
2/3 c. dark chocolate chips
1-1/2 c. whipping cream,
    divided

8-oz. pkg. reduced-fat cream
    cheese, room temperature
1/2 c. sugar
24 ladyfinger cookies
Garnish: additional baking cocoa

In a bowl, mix cocoa with hot water until dissolved; set aside. In a
small saucepan, combine chocolate chips and 1/4 cup cream; stir over
medium-low heat until melted. Remove from heat; cool to room
temperature. Transfer chocolate mixture to a large bowl; add cream
cheese and sugar. Beat with an electric mixer on low speed until
blended. Add remaining cream; beat until fluffy, about 2 minutes.
Spread 1/4 cup chocolate mixture in the bottom of an ungreased
9"x5" loaf pan. Dip 6 ladyfingers, one at a time, into cocoa mixture;
arrange in a single layer in pan. Spread 3/4 cup chocolate mixture over
ladyfingers. Repeat layering until all ladyfingers are used, ending with
remaining chocolate mixture on top. Cover and refrigerate for 2 hours
to overnight. At serving time, dust with cocoa. Makes 6 to 8 servings.

Adding chocolate curls dresses up any dessert and
they're a snap to make...just pull a vegetable peeler
over a chocolate bar and refrigerate curls until needed.

Cappuccino Mousse Trifle

Trisha Donley
Pinedale, WY

*This fluffy, light dessert is so good any time of year! It's been
a big hit at any get-together where I've served it.*

1/3 c. instant coffee granules
2-1/2 c. milk
2 3.4-oz. pkgs. instant vanilla
    pudding mix
2 8-oz. containers frozen
    whipped topping, thawed

16-oz. pkg. frozen pound cake,
    cut into 1-inch cubes
1-oz. sq. semi-sweet baking
    chocolate, grated
1/4 t. cinnamon

In a large bowl, whisk coffee granules and milk together; let stand for
5 minutes, until dissolved. Set aside one cup of coffee mixture. Add
dry pudding mixes to remaining mixture in bowl; whisk until mixture
begins to thicken. Gently fold in one container of whipped topping;
set aside. In a glass trifle bowl, layer 1/3 of cake cubes; pour 1/3 of
reserved coffee mixture evenly over cake cubes. Top with 1/3 of
pudding mixture, pressing lightly, and 1/4 of grated chocolate.
Repeat layers 2 more times; set aside
remaining grated chocolate. Spread
with remaining whipped topping,
smoothing the surface. Sprinkle with
cinnamon; add reserved grated
chocolate to center of trifle. Cover
and chill until serving time. Serves 12.

Turn your favorite cake recipe into cupcakes...terrific for school
bake sales. Fill greased muffin cups 2/3 full. Bake at the same
temperature as in the recipe, but cut the baking time by
1/3 to 1/2. From a cake recipe that makes two layers,
you'll get 24 to 30 cupcakes.

Cam's Trail Mix Cookies

Brenda Huey
Geneva, IN

A friend who's a scuba diver requested a "healthy" cookie from our bakery, and this is what we came up with. These cookies are especially good to eat on the run when you don't have time for breakfast. There's no flour in this recipe, by the way.

3 eggs, beaten
1 c. brown sugar, packed
1 c. sugar
1/2 c. margarine, softened
1-1/4 c. creamy peanut butter
1 t. corn syrup
4-1/2 c. quick-cooking oats, uncooked

2 t. baking soda
1 t. vanilla extract
1 c. assorted nuts and seeds like almonds, pecans, sunflower seeds and pumpkin seeds, chopped
1 c. assorted dried fruit, chopped

In a large bowl, stir eggs, sugars, margarine, peanut butter and corn syrup until combined. Mix in oats, baking soda and vanilla. Add remaining ingredients; stir by hand until blended. Drop dough by 1/4 cupfuls onto ungreased baking sheets, 3 inches apart. Bake at 350 degrees for 20 to 25 minutes. Cool slightly; remove to wire racks. Makes 2 dozen.

Getting a head start on your Christmas cookies? Pop up a big bowl of fresh popcorn on baking day...the kids (and you!) will have something tasty to nibble on, saving the nuts and chocolate chips for the cookies.

Save Room for Dessert

Oatmeal-Cherry Cookies

Aubrey Nygren-Earl
Taylorsville, UT

This is a nice twist on the typical oatmeal cookie...the cherries give it an extra pop of unexpected flavor! These cookies never last very long around my house.

1 c. butter, softened
1 c. brown sugar, packed
1/2 c. sugar
2 eggs, beaten
1 t. vanilla extract
1-1/2 c. all-purpose flour

1 t. baking soda
1 t. cinnamon
Optional: 1/2 t. salt
3 c. long-cooking oats,
    uncooked
1 c. sweetened dried cherries

In a large bowl, blend together butter and sugars. Add eggs and vanilla; beat well and set aside. In a separate bowl, combine flour, baking soda, cinnamon and salt, if using. Mix well and add to butter mixture. Stir in oats and cherries. Drop by rounded tablespoonfuls onto ungreased baking sheets, 2 inches apart. Bake at 350 degrees for 10 to 12 minutes, until golden. Cool for one minute on baking sheets; remove to a wire rack and cool completely. Makes 4 dozen.

Keep little ones busy and happy with a crafting area while the grown-ups put the finishing touches on Thanksgiving dinner. Set out paper plates to decorate with colored paper, feathers, pom-poms, crayons and washable glue. At dinnertime, they'll be proud to display their creations!

Old-Fashioned Sweet Potato Pie

Martha Stephens
Minden, LA

Delicious sweet potato pie was the one thing that Mama always made at Thanksgiving and Christmas. She recently passed away so now I carry on this tradition with my family.

8-oz. pkg. cream cheese, softened
1-1/4 c. sugar, divided
1/2 t. vanilla extract
3 eggs, divided
9-inch deep-dish pie crust
4 sweet potatoes, peeled, cooked and mashed
1 t. cinnamon
1/4 t. nutmeg
1/4 t. ground ginger
1/8 t. salt
1 c. evaporated milk

In a bowl, combine cream cheese, 3/4 cup sugar and vanilla; add one egg and mix well. Spread in unbaked pie crust. In a separate bowl, combine sweet potatoes, remaining sugar, spices and salt. Mix well; add remaining eggs and evaporated milk. Blend well; carefully pour over cream cheese layer. Bake at 300 degrees for 65 to 70 minutes, until set in the middle. Cool before slicing. Serves 6.

Crustless Sweet Potato Pie

Amanda Ellerbe
Santa Anna, TX

My mother gave me this recipe and I make it often. When I take this yummy pie to church, it never lasts long. I have to make two pies and sometimes that isn't enough!

4 sweet potatoes, peeled, cooked and mashed
1 c. sugar
1/2 c. all-purpose flour
1/2 c. margarine
1 egg, beaten
1/2 to 1 t. almond extract
Garnish: whipped cream

In a large bowl, combine all ingredients except garnish. Beat with an electric mixer on medium speed until well blended. Pour into a greased 9" pie plate. Bake at 450 degrees for 25 minutes. Serve warm or cooled, topped with whipped cream. Serves 6 to 8.

Save Room for
Dessert

Walnut Layer Cake

Barbara Ferree
New Freedom, PA

A church near us serves public dinners as fundraisers. We've often enjoyed the black walnut cake that's offered as one of their dessert choices. We finally tracked down the lady who makes the cake and asked if she would share her recipe. When she gave it to me, it was titled "Mother's Walnut Cake" so it is a favorite of her family as well. This is a delicious cake complemented with a wonderful cream cheese frosting.

1/2 c. butter, softened	1/2 t. salt
1/2 c. shortening	1-1/2 c. buttermilk
2 c. sugar	2 t. vanilla extract
4 eggs, beaten	1-1/2 c. plus 1/3 c. walnuts,
3-1/2 c. all-purpose flour	finely chopped
2 t. baking soda	

Blend butter, shortening and sugar in a large bowl. Add eggs; mix well and set aside. In a separate bowl, combine flour, baking soda and salt. Add flour mixture to to butter mixture alternately with buttermilk and vanilla, beating with an electric mixer on low speed just until combined. Stir in 1-1/2 cups walnuts. Pour into 3 greased and floured 9" round cake pans. Bake at 350 degrees for 35 to 40 minutes, until a toothpick tests clean. Cool in pans for 5 minutes; turn out onto a wire rack and cool completely. Assemble cake with Cream Cheese Frosting. Sprinkle with remaining walnuts. Keep refrigerated. Serves 16 to 18.

Cream Cheese Frosting:

8-oz. pkg. cream cheese, softened	3/4 c. butter, softened
3-oz. pkg. cream cheese, softened	5 to 5-1/2 c. powdered sugar
	1-1/2 t. vanilla extract

Beat cream cheese and butter in a bowl. Add sugar; mix well. Add vanilla; beat until smooth.

Grandma Mary's
Cran-Apple Stuff

Mary Anne Thomas
Salt Lake City, UT

This recipe has become a family tradition at both Thanksgiving and Christmas. The leftovers are yummy for breakfast, reheated in the microwave and topped with a little milk.

1/2 c. sugar
1/2 c. light brown sugar, packed
1 c. long-cooking oats, uncooked
3 T. all-purpose flour
1 t. cinnamon, or more to taste

1/8 t. nutmeg
1-1/2 c. fresh cranberries
3 Granny Smith apples, peeled, cored and diced
1 c. chopped walnuts
1/4 c. butter, sliced

In a bowl, combine sugars, oats, flour and spices. Add fruit and nuts; mix well. Spread in a lightly greased one-quart casserole dish; dot with butter. Bake, uncovered, at 350 degrees for 30 minutes, or until fruit is tender. Makes 8 servings.

Just-for-me mini desserts are so appealing! Bake fruit cobblers and crisps in individual ramekins...so sweet on a dinner buffet and oh-so easy for guests to serve themselves.

Mom's Jam Cookies

Connie Litfin
Carrollton, TX

My mother made these cookies as far back as I can remember. Sometimes when we got off the school bus, she would have cookies waiting for us. She always used her homemade wild strawberry jam. I like to use raspberry jam...I've been making them myself for nearly 45 years now!

1/2 c. shortening	1-2/3 c. all-purpose flour
1/3 c. sugar	1-1/2 t. baking powder
2 t. vanilla extract	Garnish: strawberry or
1 egg, beaten	raspberry jam

In a bowl, combine shortening, sugar, vanilla and egg. With an electric mixer on medium speed, beat until creamy. Stir in flour and baking powder. Drop dough by teaspoonfuls onto greased or parchment paper-lined baking sheets, one inch apart. Make a small indentation in the center of each cookie; fill each with 1/2 to 3/4 teaspoon jam. Bake at 375 degrees for 10 to 12 minutes, until edges are lightly golden. Makes 2 dozen.

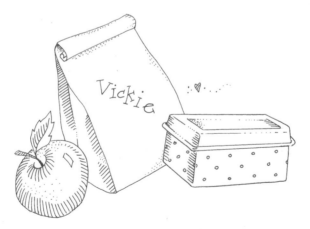

Autumn is the perfect time of year to share some tasty treats with teachers, librarians and school bus drivers...let them know how much they're appreciated!

Cherries Jubilee Crisp

Jill Valentine
Jackson, TN

I like to treat my family to a warm homemade dessert on weekends. This recipe makes just a few portions so it's sized right for small families.

17-oz. can sweet cherries
2 T. orange liqueur or
  orange juice
2-1/2 t. cornstarch
1/4 c. quick-cooking oats,
  uncooked

6 T. all-purpose flour
1/4 c. brown sugar, packed
1/4 t. nutmeg
1/4 c. cold butter, diced
Garnish: whipped cream,
  nutmeg

Combine undrained cherries, liqueur or juice and cornstarch in a saucepan. Cook and stir over medium heat until cornstarch dissolves and mixture is thickened, about 2 minutes. Pour into a lightly greased one-quart casserole dish; let cool for 10 minutes. In a small bowl, stir together oats, flour, brown sugar and nutmeg. Add butter; mix with a fork until crumbly. Sprinkle oat mixture over cherry mixture. Bake, uncovered, at 375 degrees for about 20 minutes, until topping is golden. Serve warm, topped with whipped cream and a sprinkle of nutmeg. Serves 4.

Make a trivet in a jiffy to protect the tabletop from hot dishes. Simply attach a cork or felt square to the bottom of a large ceramic tile with craft glue. It's so easy, why not make several to use on the Thanksgiving dinner table?

Save Room for Dessert

Apple-Cranberry Dump Cake
Becky Bruening
Etowah, NC

This is a scrumptious dessert for a cold autumn or winter night...
and shows that cranberries aren't just for Thanksgiving!
We love it topped with a splash of milk.

12-oz. pkg. fresh cranberries
2 Granny Smith apples, peeled,
   cored and chopped
1/2 c. chopped pecans
2/3 c. sugar

18-1/2 oz. yellow cake mix
1/2 c. butter, melted
Garnish: milk, whipped topping
   or vanilla ice cream

Place cranberries, apples and pecans in a lightly greased 13"x9" baking
pan. Sprinkle with sugar and dry cake mix; drizzle with melted butter.
Bake, uncovered, at 350 degrees for 30 to 40 minutes, until golden on
top. Serve with desired garnish. Makes 8 to 12 servings.

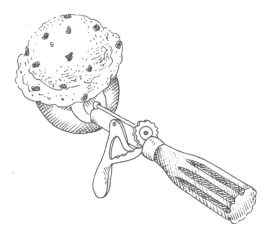

Scoops of ice cream are a perfect garnish for warm autumn pies
and puddings. Serve them in a snap...simply scoop ahead of time
into paper muffin cup liners and freeze on a baking sheet.

Saint Louie Ooey-Gooey Cake

Gwen Stutler
Emporia, KS

This is a very impressive-looking dessert for parties or company. Blueberries are my favorite, but you can use whatever kind of berries you like.

5 T. butter, melted and cooled
   slightly
1/2 c. sugar
1 egg, beaten
2/3 c. sour cream
1 c. all-purpose flour

1/2 t. baking powder
1/2 t. baking soda
1/2 c. cream cheese, softened
1-1/2 c. powdered sugar
2 c. blueberries, strawberries or
   raspberries

In a large bowl, combine butter, sugar and egg; beat together until thickened. Stir in sour cream; set aside. In a separate bowl, sift together flour, baking powder and baking soda. Add to butter mixture; beat until smooth. Pour batter into a buttered and floured 9" springform pan. Bake at 350 degrees for about 20 minutes, until cake is golden and springs back when pressed gently. Meanwhile, blend cream cheese and powdered sugar. Spread mixture over cake; arrange berries on top. Bake for an additional 25 to 30 minutes, until edges are set and center still jiggles when pan is gently shaken. Remove from oven; place pan on a wire rack and cool completely. Loosen cake from pan by running a knife around the rim; push out. Cover and chill. Bring cake back to room temperature before serving. Serves 9 to 12.

Stock up during berry-picking season for delicious desserts at Thanksgiving and Christmas. Lay unwashed berries on baking sheets and freeze, then pack into bags for the freezer. When you're ready to use them, rinse berries in a colander. They'll thaw quickly.

Save Room for Dessert

Too-Easy Toffee Cheesecake
Andrea Heyart
Aubrey, TX

This simple cheesecake is a snap to pull together,
yet tastes like you spent hours in the kitchen!

2 8-oz. pkgs. cream cheese,
    softened
2/3 c. brown sugar, packed
1 t. vanilla extract

2 eggs
1 c. chocolate-covered toffee
    baking bits, divided
9-inch graham cracker crust

In a bowl, combine cream cheese, brown sugar and vanilla. Beat with an electric mixer on medium speed until blended. Add eggs, one at a time, beating after each addition. Stir in 3/4 cup toffee bits; pour mixture into crust. Bake at 350 degrees for 35 to 40 minutes, until center is set. Sprinkle with remaining toffee bits while cheesecake is still warm. Cool; cover and refrigerate at least 3 hours. Makes 6 to 8 servings.

When our daughter was little, we used to get together with friends for a delightful evening at their farm. The older children decorated the inside of the barn and turned it into a haunted house for all to enjoy. Just before dark, we would pile onto the tractor-hitched wagon for a hayride through the woods. We always returned to a fall feast of chili, hot dogs, caramel apples and all sorts of autumn-inspired treats. Such magical memories for both kids and adults!

–Jane Wiess, Waterford, WI

Chocolate Ganache Bars

Leah Beyer
Flat Rock, IN

I love using store-bought mixes to speed up prep time on desserts. This dessert is easy to make and leaves your friends begging for the recipe! Don't be frightened by the ganache...it's just cream and chocolate.

17-1/2 oz. pkg. chocolate chip
   cookie mix
3/4 c. butter, softened and
   divided
1 egg, beaten
2 T. instant vanilla pudding mix

2 c. powdered sugar
3 T. milk
1/2 c. whipping cream
4 1-oz. sqs. semi-sweet or
   dark baking chocolate

In a bowl, combine dry cookie mix, 1/2 cup butter and egg; mix thoroughly. Spread in a lightly greased 13"x9" baking pan. Bake at 350 degrees for 20 minutes; set aside to cool completely. Melt remaining butter and add to a separate medium bowl. Stir in dry pudding mix, powdered sugar and milk. Spread over baked cookie layer. Cover and refrigerate. In a small saucepan over low heat, heat cream just to boiling; remove from heat. Add chocolate to cream; stir until completely melted. Spread over chilled pudding layer. Cover and chill to set chocolate layer. Cut into bars. Makes 2 dozen.

Bake & take! Everyone loves cookies, so set aside the day after Thanksgiving to bake up your favorites. Once all the baking and sampling is done, send family & friends home with batches of cookies to enjoy on their way.

Chocolate-Peanut Butter Marble Cake

Aqsa Masood
Ontario, Canada

I baked this cake for my son because he's fond of both peanut butter and chocolate. When I combined them just for fun, the cake came out very well...it's warm and yummy!

1 c. all-purpose flour	1/2 c. butter
1 c. sugar	5 T. canola oil
1 t. baking powder	2 eggs, beaten
1/2 t. salt	1 t. vanilla extract
1 c. semi-sweet chocolate chips,	1 c. peanut butter chips, melted
melted and cooled slightly	Optional: chocolate frosting

In a large bowl, mix flour, sugar, baking powder and salt; set aside. In a separate bowl, combine melted chocolate chips, butter, oil, eggs and vanilla; beat together. Add chocolate mixture to flour mixture. With an electric mixer on medium speed, beat for 3 minutes. Pour batter into a greased 8" round cake pan or 8"x8" baking pan. Add spoonfuls of melted peanut butter chips on top of batter; swirl through batter with a table knife. Bake at 350 degrees for 40 minutes, or until a toothpick inserted in center tests clean. Frost cake, if desired. Serves 8.

Hang a vintage wall-mounted magazine rack in the kitchen to store favorite cookbooks. Give it a fresh coat of paint in a fun color or enjoy it just as you found it.

Pumpkin Ice Cream Pie

Jackie Smulski
Lyons, IL

This dessert pie will take you from Halloween to Christmas...
a guaranteed all-around favorite.

3 c. vanilla ice cream, softened
   and divided
3 1.4-oz. toffee candy bars,
   crushed and divided
9-inch chocolate cookie crust

1/2 c. canned pumpkin
2 T. sugar
1/2 t. cinnamon
1/4 t. nutmeg

In a bowl, blend 2 cups ice cream with 2/3 of the crushed candy bars. Spoon into crust. Cover and freeze for one hour, or until firm. In a separate bowl, combine pumpkin, sugar, spices and remaining ice cream. Spread over frozen layer; top with remaining crushed candy bars. Cover and freeze for 8 hours to overnight. Remove from freezer 10 to 15 minutes before serving. Makes 8 servings.

Sweet invitations! Decorate paper gift bags with Halloween
stickers and paint...write details on one side of bag.
Later, bags can be used for collecting treats.

 Index

Appetizers

Bacon-Cheddar Cups, 176
Braunschweiger Spread, 171
Cheesy Spinach-Artichoke Dip, 177
Confetti Corn & Bean Dip, 175
Couldn't-Be-Easier Tapenade, 157
Cranberry Chicken Spread, 146
Feisty Red Pepper-Bacon Dip, 159
Firehouse Hot Meatballs, 150
Football Party Pizza Dip, 168
Game-Day Bacon-Nut Mix, 154
Game-Time Pretzels, 155
Holiday Herb Dip, 169
Hot & Sticky Maple Wings, 173
Hot Wing Dip, 172
Jim's Cheeseburger Bowl Dip, 158
Kicky Cheese Spread, 167
Laurie's Famous Bruschetta, 156
Maple-Glazed Frankies, 151
Mini Corn Quiches, 148
Pineapple Cheese Ball, 147
Poor Man's Appetizer, 157
Seasoned Spinach Balls, 149
Sneaky-Good Sausages, 151
Sweet Potato Cheese Ball, 166
Touchdown Pickle Dip, 171
Very Best Veggie Cheese, 153

Beverages

French Iced Coffee, 178
Harvest Cider, 178
Pumpkin Spice Latte, 22
Spiced Pineapple Sparkle, 163

Breads & Spreads

Apple-Walnut Muffins, 54
Brown Sugar Muffins, 11
Cheesy Beer Corn Muffins, 40
Cowpoke Cornbread, 59
Cranberry-Pumpkin Muffins, 64
Homestyle Oatmeal Bread, 53
Honey-Orange Butter, 134

Lemon-Chive Butter, 106
Luke's Baggie Bread, 47
Peach Butter Muffins, 19
Pumpkin Spice Muffins, 64

Breakfasts

Amazing Tomato Omelet, 27
Bacon & Chile Quiche, 26
Bacon-Fried Spiced Apples, 16
Camp-Time Eggs & Bacon, 17
Classic Quiche Lorraine, 23
Company Pecan French Toast, 28
Cranberry-Nut Coffee Cake, 32
Crumb Coffee Cake, 18
Farmhouse Sausage Gravy, 30
Flap Jack-o'-Lanterns, 8
Glorious Cheese Grits, 21
Goetta Breakfast Sausage, 20
Golden Banana Waffles, 9
Italian Scramble, 15
Jane's Sweet Bubble Bread, 22
Jo Ann's Garden Frittata, 14
Little Tot's Tater Breakfast, 24
Mashed Potato Doughnuts, 13
Mom's Buttermilk Pancakes, 12
Mom's Orange Bow Knots, 33
Nutty Skillet Granola, 34
Poached Eggs & Grits, 31
Roz's Brunch Casserole, 6
Ruby's B&B Spinach Quiche, 35
Sausage Balls, 29
Scrambled Egg Muffins, 10
Sunny-Side-Up Egg Pizza, 25
Sweet Blintz Soufflé, 29
Touchdown Doughnut Balls, 179
Ursula's Breakfast Danish, 7
Wilderness Breakfast, 16

Cookies & Candy

Autumn Pumpkin Bars, 193
Cam's Trail Mix Cookies, 206
Chocolate Ganache Bars, 216
Cranberry-Orange Drops, 199

Index

Frosted Pumpkin Cookies, 196
Glazed Apple Cookies, 198
Halloween Popcorn Balls, 180
Jumbo Candy Cookies, 195
Mom's Jam Cookies, 211
Oatmeal-Cherry Cookies, 207
Orange Gingerbread Cut-Outs, 197
Raisin Squares, 203
Walnut Frosties, 192

Desserts

Apple-Cranberry Dump Cake, 213
Brown Sugar Nut Pie, 188
Buttermilk Pear Cobbler, 190
Cappuccino Mousse Trifle, 205
Caramel Apple Cake, 185
Cheddar Crumble Apple Pie, 191
Cherries Jubilee Crisp, 212
Chocolate-Bacon Cupcakes, 194
Chocolate-Peanut Butter Marble
    Cake, 217
Country Harvest Pie, 189
Cranberry Frappe, 105
Crustless Sweet Potato Pie, 208
Double Chocolate Tiramisu, 204
Ginger Ale Baked Apples, 103
Gingersnap Pumpkin Pie, 183
Grandma Mary's Cran-Apple
    Stuff, 210
Grandma's Cherry Pudding Cake, 188
Halloween Poke Cake, 184
Heavenly Key Lime Pie, 200
Hot Lemon Pie, 200
Lemon Upside-Down Cake, 201
Old-Fashioned Sweet Potato Pie, 208
Pumpkin Ice Cream Pie, 218
Rose's Black Midnight Cake, 187
Saint Louie Ooey-Gooey Cake, 214
Signature Chocolate Cream Pie, 186
Too-Easy Toffee Cheesecake, 215
Upside-Down Apple-Pecan Pie, 182
Vi's Fruit Cocktail Cake, 202
Walnut Layer Cake, 209

Mains

Bratwurst Meatloaf, 120
Brown Sugar Glazed Ham, 110
Caraway Pot Roast, 128
Cheeseburger Macaroni, 81
Cheesy Chili Dog Bake, 95
Creamy Chicken & Broccoli, 86
Crunchy Turkey Casserole, 136
Delicious Bacon Turkey, 122
Delicious Creamed Turkey, 137
Easy Stuffed Manicotti, 96
Family-Favorite Mac & Cheese, 138
Favorite Apricot Chicken, 100
Gobble-Good Turkey Bake, 98
Grandma's Spaghetti Supreme, 76
Grandma's Special Pork Chops, 89
Grilled Lemon Turkey, 72
Halloween Hash, 77
Harvest-Time Pork Loin, 112
Hearty Beef Macaroni, 94
Holiday Brined Turkey, 108
Honey-Garlic Drumsticks, 78
Lazy Lasagna, 97
Macaroni Cheese Twists, 84
Mom's Mexican Mess, 85
No-Noodle Eggplant Lasagna, 114
Oh-So-Good Crispy Chicken, 78
Roasted Chicken Sausage
    & Potatoes, 71
Saucy Barbecue Hens, 115
Sausage & Apple Kraut, 70
Savory Pork Roast, 102
Sofie's Upside-Down Hamburger
    Pie, 80
Tasty Turkey Roll-Ups, 74
Thyme Pork Chops, 88
Turkey Croquettes, 130

Salads

Almond-Orange Salad, 133
Apple & Orange Slaw, 101
Arugula Salad & Baked Pears, 132
Aunt Patty's Pea Salad, 142

Broccoli Salad Supreme, 143
Cranberry Orchard Salad, 144
Cranberry-Pear Tossed Salad, 99
Crunchy Cashew Slaw, 140
Feta Cheese Tossed Salad, 104
Sandra's Pomegranate Salad, 141
Spirited Cherry Salad, 135

Sandwiches

Brisket Roll Sandwiches, 174
Budget Turkey Sandwiches, 90
Cranberry BBQ Pork Rolls, 164
Curried Chicken Party Rolls, 152
Game-Day Subs, 170
Italian Hamburgers, 160
Mom's Chili Dogs, 161
Secret Sandwich for a Crowd, 162

Sides

Asparagus Bundles, 113
Barbecue Green Beans, 126
Braised Cabbage & Apples, 121
Broccoli-Corn Casserole, 124
Brown Sugar-Bacon Squash, 117
Buttery Cabbage & Noodles, 79
Caesar Green Beans, 126
Carrots & Cheese Casserole, 118
Corn & Spinach Casserole, 92
Corn, Lima & Tomato Bake, 125
Cranberry Fruit Conserve, 134
Creamy Skillet Corn, 82
Easy Cheesy Potatoes, 89
Easy Ranch Potatoes, 75
Garlicky Broccoli & Pasta, 83
Gingery Glazed Carrots, 93
Granny's Cornbread Dressing, 109
Grilled Sweet Potato Fries, 73
Hazel's Stuffing Balls, 131
Herb-Buttered Broccoli, 82
Herbed Potato Gratin, 122

Icebox Mashed Potatoes, 123
Maple Baked Beans, 116
Orange & Honey Yams, 129
Parmesan Potatoes, 139
Pumpkin Hollow Surprise, 36
Roasted Brussels Sprouts, 113
Sally's Broccoli Puff, 127
Scalloped Celery, 119
Slow-Cooked Stadium Beans, 165
Sweet Potatoes in Baskets, 111
Twice-Baked Sweet Potatoes, 91

Soups & Stews

Bean & Butternut Soup, 39
Chicken & Barley Soup, 45
Chicken Enchilada Soup, 61
Chourico & Kale Soup, 56
Creamy Corn Bisque, 57
Creamy Turkey Soup, 42
Dad Cole's Hearty Beef Stew, 52
Darlene's 5-Can Beef Stew, 87
Feel-Better Chicken Soup, 65
Fiery Tortilla Soup, 44
Hungarian Beef Soup, 63
Indian Corn Stew, 38
Italian Sausage-Zucchini Soup, 60
Karen's Fish Chowder, 51
Kitchen Cupboard Soup, 66
Mashed Potato & Turkey Soup, 43
Mémère's Vegetable Soup, 49
Mom's Beef Vegetable Soup, 46
My Best Bean & Bacon Soup, 58
Nanny Newman's Chili, 46
Oh-So-Easy Chili, 40
Parmesan Potato Soup, 55
Pork Stew & Dumplin's, 62
Portuguese Pea Stew, 48
Satisfying Slim-Down Soup, 68
Savory Onion & Garlic Soup, 67
Slow-Cooked Campfire Stew, 41
Tangy Salmon Cream Soup, 50

Have a taste for more?

We created our official Circle of Friends so we could
fill everyone in on the latest scoop at once.
Visit us online to join in the fun and discover free
recipes, exclusive giveaways and much more!

www.gooseberrypatch.com

Call us toll-free at 1·800·854·6673

U.S. to Canadian recipe equivalents

Volume Measurements

1/4 teaspoon	1 mL
1/2 teaspoon	2 mL
1 teaspoon	5 mL
1 tablespoon = 3 teaspoons	15 mL
2 tablespoons = 1 fluid ounce	30 mL
1/4 cup	60 mL
1/3 cup	75 mL
1/2 cup = 4 fluid ounces	125 mL
1 cup = 8 fluid ounces	250 mL
2 cups = 1 pint =16 fluid ounces	500 mL
4 cups = 1 quart	1 L

Weights

1 ounce	30 g
4 ounces	120 g
8 ounces	225 g
16 ounces = 1 pound	450 g

Oven Temperatures

300° F	150° C
325° F	160° C
350° F	180° C
375° F	190° C
400° F	200° C
450° F	230° C

Baking Pan Sizes

Square

8x8x2 inches	2 L = 20x20x5 cm
9x9x2 inches	2.5 L = 23x23x5 cm

Rectangular

13x9x2 inches	3.5 L = 33x23x5 cm

Loaf

9x5x3 inches	2 L = 23x13x7 cm

Round

8x1-1/2 inches	1.2 L = 20x4 cm
9x1-1/2 inches	1.5 L = 23x4 cm